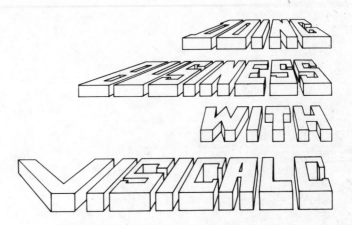

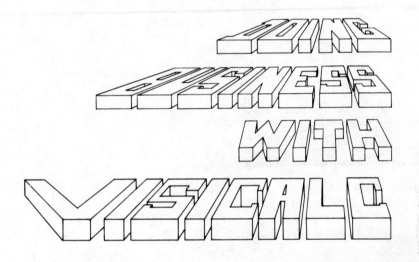

Doing Business with Visicalc

Stanley R. Trost

Berkeley • Paris • Düsseldorf

Cover art by Daniel Le Noury
Layout and design by Ingrid Owen.

Apple is a registered trademark of Apple Computer, Inc.
DIF is a trademark of Software Arts, Inc.
IBM is a registered trademark of International Business Machines Corporation.
Silentype is a trademark of Apple Computer, Inc.
TRS-80 is a trademark of Tandy Corporation.
VisiCalc is a registered trademark of VisiCorp, Inc.
VisiPlot is a registered trademark of VisiCorp, Inc.

Library of Congress Card Number: 82-50622
ISBN 0-89588-086-5
Printed in the United States of America
10 9 8 7 6 5 4 3

To Elaine

ACKNOWLEDGEMENTS

The following individuals and organizations were very helpful to me in the development of this book:

Dr. Rudolph Langer
Salley Oberlin
Joel Kreisman
Sybex, Inc.
VisiCorp
Richard Melmon
Dr. Willard Wattenburg
John Huebell

TABLE OF CONTENTS

8 INCOME TAXES

INTRODUCTION

The VisiCalc® program is one of the best-known and most popular application programs for personal computers. This impressive software tool can turn your computer into an "electronic spreadsheet" that will perform hundreds of calculations in only minutes. Yet learning to use this powerful program is scarcely harder than learning to use a simple pocket calculator.

Doing Business with VisiCalc is a quick and easy guide to using the VisiCalc program for performing common business calculations. This book presents over forty planning and forecasting applications, ranging from financial statements to master budgets, and pricing models to investment strategies. Each application is described in detail, and a complete "program" for setting up the application in VisiCalc notation is presented.

In preparing the examples for this book, the author has assumed that the reader has an introductory-level understanding of the VisiCalc program. For those readers who wish to refresh their memory, the author has provided an appendix that includes a complete summary of the VisiCalc conventions and commands.

Many of the programs presented in this book can be used directly to meet individual business needs, or they can be easily modified to meet specific requirements. The goal of this book, then, is twofold:

1. to present a collection of VisiCalc programs that can be applied to business

2. to guide the VisiCalc user toward an advanced level of familiarity with this tremendously powerful tool.

CONTENTS

Chapter 1 introduces the basic definitions and concepts of the VisiCalc program. It describes specific features of the program; reviews the use of formulas; provides information on form layout; and discusses printing techniques. In addition, it describes a new concept designed by the author for preparing and presenting spreadsheet instructions.

Chapter 2 produces VisiCalc spreadsheets for record-keeping applications. You will learn to prepare a sales register, a check ledger, two types of invoices, and a basic income statement. Examples are explained in detail, so that you can become more familiar with using the VisiCalc program.

Chapter 3 develops an extensive set of tools—including a comparative income statement and a balance sheet—for analyzing financial data; you will then see how these statements can be combined into a report for analyzing key business ratios. You will also learn how to prepare a depreciation schedule, and you will develop several spreadsheets that use discounted cash flow analyses for comparing alternative investments.

Chapter 4 prepares a complete budgeting system for a small company. Starting with a sales and manufacturing budget, you will create a projected income statement, and several cash plans.

Chapter 5 uses the VisiCalc program to predict and analyze sales. It builds several forecasting models based on compound growth, seasonal variation, mathematical models, and linear regression, and prepares tools for evaluating product contribution and individual sales performance. Several examples demonstrate the usefulness of graphs for presenting spreadsheet information.

Chapter 6 develops VisiCalc application examples for manufacturing situations. In addition to providing several record-keeping examples, it shows you how to track quality control, prepare inventory analyses, develop learning curve applications, and prepare a hiring plan.

Chapter 7 creates VisiCalc spreadsheets for real estate applications. You will learn to prepare a mortgage payment schedule, a depreciation schedule that handles component depreciation, and other tools for analyzing real estate investments.

Chapter 8 uses the VisiCalc program to implement several federal income tax forms. In particular, it demonstrates the VisiCalc "What if" function for tax planning purposes.

A complete review of the conventions and commands of the VisiCalc program is presented in Appendix A. Appendix B considers additional features incorporated in the VisiCalc Advanced Version.

As a final note, all of the examples in this book have been validated on an Apple® II, TRS-80™, and an IBM® Personal Computer.

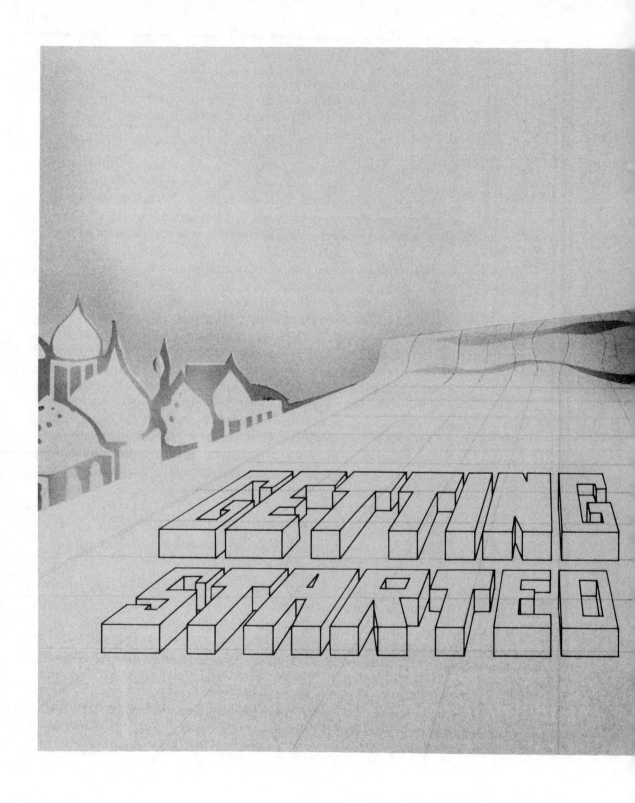

1
GETTING STARTED

OVERVIEW

In this chapter we will explore many of the basic features of the VisiCalc program. We will learn how to tabulate and display information on a VisiCalc spreadsheet, and we will review many important definitions and terms. In addition, we will look at a new method developed by the author that can be used to prepare VisiCalc documentation.

An important premise of this book is that, to be easily understood, information must be presented legibly. We will therefore examine several useful techniques for designing and producing neat, well-organized, professional-looking reports.

THE BASICS OF THE VISICALC PROGRAM

Figure 1.1 displays a short report printed by the VisiCalc program. This report shows the effect of compounding $1,000 at 5% and 10% per annum for four years. To understand how this report was produced, we will now review and examine some of the basic features of a VisiCalc spreadsheet display.

	A	B	C	D	E
1		COMPOUND	GROWTH		
2	RATE %	1981	1982	1983	1984
3	5	1000	1050	1102.50	1157.63
4	10	1000	1100	1210	1331

Figure 1.1: A Short Report

THE SPREADSHEET

The VisiCalc program can maintain up to 254 rows and 63 columns of information, depending on your computer's memory size. In VisiCalc, the rows are numbered from 1 to 254 and the columns from A to BK (i.e., A–Z, AA–AZ and BA–BK). Figure 1.1 shows a VisiCalc display of four rows (1 through 4) and five columns (A through E). A *coordinate* is the intersection of a row and a column. For example, in Figure 1.1 the coordinate C1 shows the word GROWTH, and the coordinate E4 contains the number 1331.

The coordinates on a VisiCalc display can hold one of three types of entries: labels, values or variables. Generally, a *label* heads a row or column and "labels" the tabular data (the values and variables) in that row or column. In the example in Figure 1.1, the years 1981, 1982, 1983, and 1984 are labels. The title, COMPOUND GROWTH, is also a label. Note that a label may consist of numbers or letters.

A *value* is a number typed in by the user. In Figure 1.1, the percentages 5 and 10, located at the coordinates A3 and A4, are values.

A *variable* is a quantity that is calculated from a formula. For example, the formula

$$C3:(1+(A3/100))*B3$$

produces the variable 1050 (see Figure 1.2). (We discuss formulas in detail in a later section.)

To generate a spreadsheet display, we first load the VisiCalc program. Then we specify a sequence of instructions to the program and enter the data. The VisiCalc program then combines the data and instructions to produce a spreadsheet. (In Figure 1.1 and throughout this book, we have displayed *user-entered data* in **boldface** type.)

Let's now examine the sequence of VisiCalc instructions that produced the report in Figure 1.1. We refer to this sequence as the *spreadsheet instructions*.

SPREADSHEET INSTRUCTIONS

Figure 1.2 shows the spreadsheet instructions for the COMPOUND GROWTH example. We have prepared all spreadsheet instructions in this book using the following conventions:

- We use a letter, a number, and a colon to represent the coordinate position into which the label, value or formula that follows, is to be typed. For example, the instruction

  B2:1981

  instructs you to move the cursor to coordinate B2 and enter the value 1981. (You must then press the RETURN or ENTER key to enter the data.)

- The slash character indicates to the VisiCalc program that the instruction that follows the slash is a program instruction. For example, /CY tells the program that it should "clear the display."

```
/CY
B1:/FR COMPOUND    C1:/FR GROWTH
A2:/FR RATE %
B2:/FI
/R:C2.E2
B2:1981
   B3:1000
   B4:1000
C2:1982              D2:1983              E2:1984
   C3:(1+(A3/100))*B3
   /R:D3.E3:NR
   C4:(1+(A4/100))*B4
   /R:D4.E4:NR
```

Figure 1.2: Spreadsheet Instructions: COMPOUND GROWTH

We have also used a method known as *structured documentation* to prepare the spreadsheet instructions. We will now examine this method.

Structured Documentation

Over the years, computer scientists have worked to develop alternative documentation techniques, in conjunction with their search for better programming methods and languages. This has led to the development of several languages, such as Pascal and ADA, and to numerous refinements in the use of existing languages. One of the most powerful techniques that has evolved from this search is a method known as *structured program design*. This design advocates the use of top-down structuring, highly-modular code and easily-identifiable mnemonics.

In the spreadsheet documentation for the examples in this book, we have incorporated several principles postulated by Brian Kernighan and P.J. Plauger[1], and Dennie Van Tassel[2]. These include:

- using parentheses (they are cheaper than errors)
- formatting a program so that it can be easily understood
- using indentation to show program structure.

If you follow these principles when you prepare your VisiCalc instructions, it will be easier for you to produce spreadsheet instructions that work correctly the first time and documentation that can be easily read and understood by others. Let's examine Figure 1.2 and see the usefulness of structured documentation.

Preparing the Spreadsheet

Let's go over the spreadsheet instructions in Figure 1.2, line by line. In the first line, we specify:

    /CY

The /C instruction tells VisiCalc to clear the screen and memory, and the Y acknowledges the program prompt, "Type Y to confirm."

---

[1] Brian W. Kernighan and P. J. Plauger, *The Elements of Programming Style*, (New York: McGraw-Hill, 1974), pp. 121–127.

[2] Dennie Van Tassel, *Program Style, Design, Efficiency, Debugging and Testing*, (Englewood Cliffs, New Jersey: Prentice Hall, 1978), p. 33.

In the next line:

    B1:/FR COMPOUND   C1:/FR GROWTH

we specify that the spreadsheet title is to be located at coordinates B1 and C1.

In the following line:

    A2:/FR RATE %

we specify that the label, RATE %, is to appear in coordinate A2 in a right-justified format.

Similarly, the label and notation:

    B2:/FI
    /R: C2.E2
    B2:1981
        B3:1000
        B4:1000

indicate that the starting amounts in 1981 are both $1,000. We use the command /FI to put the label 1981 in integer format and the /R command to replicate this format for the labels in coordinates C2, D2, and E2. We indent B3 and B4 to indicate that the $1,000 amounts belong with the year 1981.

Next, we write the headings for the remaining years and give the formulas for the data:

    C2:1982   D2:1983   E2:1984
        C3:(1+(A3/100))*B3
        /R:D3.E3:NR
        C4:(1+(A4/100))*B4
        /R:D4.E4:NR

The indented formulas at C3 and C4 indicate that they belong with the preceding labels: 1982, 1983, and 1984. The formula at C3 divides the percentage at A3 by 100 (to put it into decimal notation), adds a 1 (to put it into compound interest form), and then multiplies the result by the initial amount at B3 (to calculate the new value). The formula at C4 is similar to the one at C3.

Note that the specification:

    C3:(1+(A3/100))*B3
    /R:D3.E3:NR

is read in the following way:

1. Move the cursor to C3, and enter the formula:

   (1+(A3/100))*B3

2. Leave the cursor at C3, and replicate the formula by typing:

   /R:D3.E3:NR

Let's now look at another example that adds a new dimension to the preparation of a VisiCalc spreadsheet. Figure 1.3 shows the spreadsheet for a sales forecast that makes use of a *parameter table*. A parameter table is an easy method for storing program variables and is, therefore, very useful in the preparation of Visi-Calc spreadsheets. The spreadsheet instructions for the sales forecast in Figure 1.3 appear in Figure 1.4.

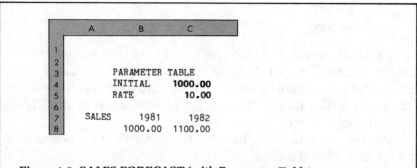

```
         A         B         C
1
2
3              PARAMETER  TABLE
4              INITIAL    1000.00
5              RATE         10.00
6
7    SALES       1981      1982
8              1000.00   1100.00
```

Figure 1.3: SALES FORECAST (with Parameter Table)

```
/CY
/GF$
B3:PARAMETER        C3:" TABLE
   B4:INITIAL       C4:1000
   B5:RATE          C5:10
A7:SALES
   B7:/FI 1981      C7:/FI 1982
      B8:+C4
      C8:(1+(C5/100))*B8
```

Figure 1.4: Spreadsheet Instructions: SALES FORECAST

In Figure 1.4, we enter the initial data—the sales amount and sales growth rate—in a parameter table. Because we have grouped the program variables together at the beginning of the spreadsheet, we can easily change them, and then quickly and easily review the effects of these changes.

The example in Figure 1.4 calculates the sales figures for the years 1981 and 1982. In 1981, the sales figure is copied directly out of the parameter table. In 1982, it is computed by using the formula in coordinate C8.

The use of formulas for producing output is an important asset of the VisiCalc program. When preparing formulas for the VisiCalc program we must adhere to some important procedures that we will now discuss.

The Use of Formulas

A few words of caution are in order here regarding the use of formulas. In the VisiCalc program, formula calculation is done on a strict left-to-right basis, with the exception of those cases where quantities are placed inside parentheses. *Note: quantities placed inside parentheses are always computed first. Beware:* It is easy to obtain false results if you are not careful. Let's look at an example.

Throughout this book we often use the formula for compound interest with the percentage expressed as a whole amount. The following sequence converts the percentage to a decimal:

A1:RATE %	B1:10
A2:AMOUNT	B2:1000
A3:GROWTH	

B3:(1+(B1/100))*B2

In the expression at B3, the division by 100 must occur inside parentheses (i.e., it must be computed first) to generate the correct result.

As written, the formula for B3 would be evaluated by the VisiCalc program to produce the result

B3: 1100

Omission of the second set of parentheses would produce an incorrect result, i.e.,

B3: 110

We suggest that you use parentheses liberally with your formulas to avoid errors.

We will now examine methods for laying out spreadsheets.

FORM LAYOUT

It is possible that many of the reports that you will be generating with the VisiCalc program will be important documents that will be used and reviewed by other people. In this section, we will show you how you can prepare neat, well-organized, professional-looking reports.

Figure 1.5 shows a typical report generated by the VisiCalc program—an income projection for an office building. We will not discuss here how the report was produced—the actual spreadsheet instructions appear in Chapter 7—instead, we will use this report to point out the basic features of the VisiCalc program.

Title And Date

Let's begin by carefully examining the report in Figure 1.5. Looking at the top of the report, we can see that the title and preparation date are centered above the body of the report. Since the examples in this book are designed for an 80-column printer (i.e., they use eight columns of nine characters each), to center a title on a page, we must enter the title in the center columns; in this case, columns C and D. (Note, however, that the columns C and D would not be correct for a report that contains fewer than eight columns.) Since the column width can restrict the way a title is printed, some care must be taken when entering a title. For example, for the spreadsheets in this book, if a word in a title is longer than nine characters, we must split it between two columns. As an example, we create the title "CONDO INVESTMENT" by specifying:

C5:CONDO   D5:INVESTMEN   E5:T

Labels

Note that the spreadsheet in Figure 1.5 is divided into two halves by a dashed line. The upper half is a parameter table, consisting of labels (SALES PRICE, DOWN PAYMENT, etc.) and data (125,000; 25,000, etc.). The lower half contains the report.

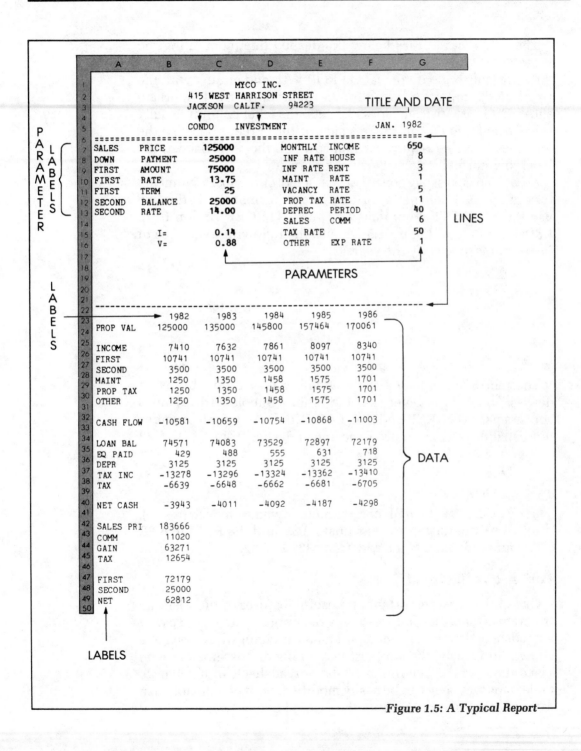

Figure 1.5: A Typical Report

The row that appears below the dashed line (containing the years 1982–1986), and the column that runs down the left side of the page (starting with the label PROP VAL and ending with the word NET), contain the labels for the report portion of the spreadsheet. On most VisiCalc spreadsheets, the label column usually starts in column A, on the left side of the screen. Because the variables and title require several rows on the spreadsheet, the label row normally starts at row 5 or greater.

Recall that labels may consist of characters or numbers. Numbers used as labels should be put in local integer format. To do this, we use the FORMAT command and the INTEGER option (/FI). In the example in Figure 1.5, we use the following sequence of instructions to specify the years:

```
A23:/FI
/R:B23.F23
B23:1982          C23:1983          D23:1984
E23:1985          F23:1986
```

Lines

You can often enhance the readability of a report by using dashes, equal signs, asterisks, and other symbols to draw lines across a page. The REPEATING LABEL (/−) command provides this capability. Thus, to draw the line of dashes from A22 to G22 in Figure 1.5, we write:

```
A22:/− −
/R:B22.G22
```

The REPEATING LABEL command followed by a dash (/− −), draws a row of dashes in coordinate A22, and the REPLICATE (/R) command extends the row from B22 to G22.

Parameters Revisited

One of the most important and useful features of the VisiCalc program is that it can automatically recompute and produce new spreadsheet data whenever a parameter is changed. As we have shown previously, the simplest way to handle parameters is to place them at the beginning of the spreadsheet, in a separate table. This way they can be easily modified, or, if you do not wish to display them, omitted from the printed copy.

. In the example in Figure 1.5, the parameter table appears between the row of equal signs and the row of dashes. When we print this report, we can exclude this table, if we wish, by starting the printing below the parameter table. For example, we can print the entire report by placing the cursor at A1 and typing:

        /PP

        G50

Or, we can eliminate the parameter table and print only the projection, by positioning the cursor at A23 and typing:

        /PP

        G50

Data

The main body of the report contains the data, which is either entered directly by the user, or computed from formulas. Since most of the examples in this book are business examples, we often use the GLOBAL $ FORMAT (/GF$) command to specify the data. When preparing the spreadsheet instructions for such examples, it is important to include this command early in the specifications—prior to the establishment of any local formats. To do this, we write:

        /GF$

If, however, after using this command, we enter any digits that represent years, zip codes, etc., we must remember to put them in local integer format or to precede them with the quotation symbol ("), so that the /GF$ command will not append a decimal.

Order of Computing

The normal order of computing in VisiCalc is to proceed down the columns and then across the rows. More explicitly, the VisiCalc program computes A1, A2, and so on, up to A254; then it moves to B1, B2, etc., finishing at B254. It is important to remember this order of computing when preparing spreadsheet instructions. Non-compliance with this order may lead to unreliable results.

As an example, the @SUM function is normally used to add columns. Even though in some cases it may be desirable to enter the total at the top of the column, proper computing order dictates that the total appear at the bottom. It is possible to compute in row order by using the GLOBAL ORDER command (/GOR).

Precision

The VisiCalc program stores numbers internally in binary computer form. These stored numbers have a high degree of precision—the VisiCalc program can calculate and round-off numbers up to 11 and sometimes 12 decimal places. However, when results appear on the computer screen, or are printed out by a printer, rounding errors can take place.

We can obtain correct results up to two decimal places with the following formula:

$$@INT((COORD)*100+.5))/100$$

In this formula, COORD represents the location where we wish to increase the precision. When applying this formula, it may not be necessary to apply it to every coordinate; instead, we may only want to use it for column totals. For example, if we want to obtain a column sum at location B30, we might enter the following formula:

$$B30:@INT(B29*100+.5))/100$$

Printer Width

Obviously, the number of characters that a printer can print in a row will affect the format of a report. Since most printers are eighty characters wide, we have formatted the reports in this book to meet that requirement.

Paste-Up

There will be times when the report you wish to produce simply will not coincide with the width of your printer. Recall that the VisiCalc program is internally capable of maintaining 63 columns; however, because of the way we have formatted the reports in the book, we can only print out 8 columns at a time. Therefore, if we are printing a report that has more than 8 columns, we must print the report in sections, and then use scissors and glue to produce the desired completed report. *Note:* don't forget to center your title across the final pasted form.

Column Width

The default column width in the VisiCalc program is 9 characters. You can, however, obtain more columns per page, by using the GLOBAL COLUMN (/GC) command. This command reduces the (global) column width, and frees space for additional columns. (*Note:* The standard 9 character width will print a number as large as 99999999.)

Now that we have discussed the basic features of the VisiCalc program that help us design more readable reports, let's examine some useful methods for laying out more complex formats.

Layout of Complex Reports

The VisiCalc program is designed to help you create reports interactively on a CRT screen. The author recommends that you sketch out a spreadsheet report prior to entering it on the CRT screen. This will help you produce more readable and reliable reports.

Figure 1.6 shows a report that was previously sketched out. To

	1 A	2 B	3 C	4 D	5 E	6
1			P + L			
2						
3		Jan.	Feb.	Mar.	YTD	
4	Sales				S(B4.D4)	
5	Cost				S(B5.D5)	
6	G.P.	B4 - B5	C4 - C5	D4 - D5	S(B6.D6)	
7						
8	G + A					
9	Selling					
10						
11	Net	B6-B8-B9	C6-C8-C9	D6-D8-D9	S(B11.D11)	
12						
13						
14						

Figure 1.6: Spreadsheet Preparation Form

transfer these instructions to the VisiCalc program, you do the following:

- First, you enter the labels onto the screen, by transferring them coordinate-by-coordinate from the layout to the CRT.
- Next, you type in the formulas.
- Finally, you enter the variables.

By sketching out a spreadsheet entry form prior to entering the spreadsheet on the computer, you can more easily see the line up of the rows and columns, check for forward references, and write down and prepare important formulas.

A MASTER FORM

If you plan to use the VisiCalc program to create a series of reports or forms for a business, you may want to create and maintain a master form that contains the name and address of your firm, as well as other pertinent information. You can then store this master form as a VisiCalc file on disk, and recall it prior to specifying each new spreadsheet display. By doing this, you can avoid re-entering the same information over and over again.

For the examples in this book, we have developed a master form for MYCO, Inc. We have stored this form as the file, MASTER.VC. (*Note:* the VisiCalc program for the IBM Personal Computer does not require the use of the file extension .VC. Therefore, if you are using IBM VisiCalc, store this file as MASTER.)

In this book, each time we create a new report, we will simply clear the VisiCalc memory and then load this master file. To do this, we type:

    /CY

    /SL MASTER.VC

The specifications for this master form are:

D1:MYCO INC.		
C2:"415 WEST	D2:HARRISON	E2:STREET
C3:JACKSON	D3:CALIF.	E3:"94223
D5:**TITLE**	G5:**DATE**	
A6:/ — =		
/R:B6.H6		

An example of our master form appears in Figure 1.7. As we use this form with each new spreadsheet, we will replace the "TITLE" and "DATE" labels with the appropriate information.

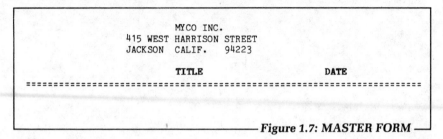

```
                          MYCO INC.
               415 WEST HARRISON STREET
         JACKSON   CALIF.   94223

                         TITLE                          DATE
========================================================================
```

Figure 1.7: MASTER FORM

SUMMARY

This introductory chapter has given a step-by-step description of the process involved in specifying and setting up a VisiCalc spreadsheet. You should now be ready to proceed to the following chapters and use the VisiCalc program for a number of useful applications.

2
RECORD-KEEPING

Sales Register Check Register
Expense Register Invoice
Income Statement

OVERVIEW

In this chapter we will develop VisiCalc spreadsheets for several record-keeping applications. To help you better understand the VisiCalc program, as well as the methodology and documentation used throughout this book, detailed explanations are given with each example.

We will begin by using the VisiCalc program to prepare a spreadsheet for a simple sales register. We will then construct a complete check register—one that is useful for both personal and business applications—and modify it to create an expense register.

Next, we will develop a complete sales invoice and use the @LOOKUP and @IF functions—two important functions of the VisiCalc program.

In the last example, we will develop a yearly income statement, and use the file transfer capability of the VisiCalc program to post expense ledger entries from a monthly to a yearly journal.

This chapter is designed to help you increase your knowledge of the VisiCalc program. The examples we present range from the very simple—a simple sales register— to the more complex and sophisticated—a yearly income statement. You should be able to easily adapt these examples and use them in many situations. The VisiCalc program can eliminate the need for additional specialized software.

SALES REGISTER

We will begin by using the VisiCalc program to design a sales register. We start with this example because it is relatively simple and introduces many of the concepts that we will be using throughout this book.

APPLICATION EXAMPLE

Let's assume that you own a small bakery that sells to both wholesale and retail customers. You want to record your sales on a daily basis. For wholesale transactions you plan to record the invoice number, the date of the sale, the customer's name, and the amount of the sale. For retail sales you plan to enter daily sales figures from a cash register tape. You want to compute monthly totals; and you plan to initiate a new register each month.

SPREADSHEET DESIGN

The easiest way to plan the layout for this type of display is to sketch out a design on a sample VisiCalc spreadsheet and then add sample data. Figure 2.1 shows a preliminary layout for this example. In this figure, we can see that the "SOLD TO" column must be wider than we had originally planned. We must use a double column. In addition, to ensure that the invoice numbers do not overlap the customer names, we must use the LEFT FORMAT (/FL) command. (*Remember*: labels are automatically left-justified, and numbers right-justified.)

A corrected and completed spreadsheet appears in Figure 2.2. We can use this spreadsheet to compute the net sales figures by adding the sales tax to the amount of sales. The spreadsheet instructions for this display appear in Figure 2.3.

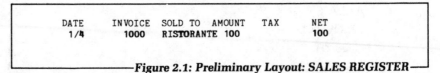

DATE	INVOICE	SOLD TO	AMOUNT	TAX	NET
1/4	1000	RISTORANTE	100		100

Figure 2.1: Preliminary Layout: SALES REGISTER

```
         A        B        C        D        E        F        G
 1                              MYCO INC.
 2                    415 WEST HARRISON STREET
 3                    JACKSON   CALIF.   94223
 4
 5                    SALES     REGISTER                  JAN. 1982
 6  =================================================================
 7  DATE    INVOICE  SOLD TO               AMOUNT     TAX        NET
 8   1/4    1000     BLUE FOX              100.00              100.00
 9   1/4    1001     OSCARS                 75.00               75.00
10   1/4    1002     DOROS                  60.00               60.00
11   1/4    1003     ERNIES                125.00              125.00
12   1/4             CASH                  351.40   22.84      374.24
13   1/5    1004     BLUE FOX               90.00               90.00
14   1/5    1005     DOROS                  85.00               85.00
15   1/5    1006     ERNIES                130.00              130.00
16   1/5             CASH                  303.39   19.72      323.11
17   1/6    1007     DOROS                 120.00              120.00
18   1/6    1008     OSCARS                 80.00               80.00
19   1/6    1009     BLUE FOX               70.00               70.00
20                                                              0.00
21                                                              0.00
22                                                              0.00
23                                                              0.00
24                                                              0.00
25                                                              0.00
26                                                              0.00
27                                                              0.00
28                                                              0.00
29                                                              0.00
30  -------------------------------------------------------------
31                    TOTALS             1589.79   42.56     1632.35
```

Figure 2.2: SALES REGISTER

SPREADSHEET INSTRUCTIONS

Let's now refer to Figure 2.3 and examine each instruction.

```
/CY
/SL MASTER.VC
/GF$
    C5:SALES              D5:REGISTER           G5:JAN. 1982
    A7:DATE
    B7:INVOICE
      B8:/FL
      /R:B9.B29
    C7:SOLD TO
    E7:/FR
    /R:F7.G7
    E7:AMOUNT             F7:TAX
    G7:NET
      G8:+E8+F8
      /R:G9.G29:RR
    A30:/——
    /R:B30.G30
    D31:TOTALS
      E31:@SUM(E8.E29)
      /R:F31.G31:RR
```

Figure 2.3: Spreadsheet Instructions: SALES REGISTER

We begin the spreadsheet instructions by writing

    /CY
    /SL MASTER.VC
    /GF$

The first instruction, /CY, performs five tasks. It erases any current information from the computer memory, sets the default global formats, returns the cursor to the home position, sets the order of calculation to column, and enables automatic recalculation as data is entered.

Note: depending on the computer system you are using, you will need to press either the RETURN or ENTER key after entering each instruction.

The next instruction, /SL MASTER.VC, loads into the computer memory the master form that we developed in Chapter 1. The instruction /GF$ ensures that all data appear in dollar and cents format (i.e., that the data appear with two figures to the right of the decimal point).

Next, we enter the labels and formulas that specify the spreadsheet layout. The instructions:

     C5:SALES   D5:REGISTER   G5:JAN. 1982

create the form title and date.

The column heading for the date is:

     A7:DATE

We enter the invoice numbers in column B. To make a more readable report, we left-justify the invoice numbers. Thus:

     B7:INVOICE
       B8:/FL
       /R:B9.B29

Next, we enter the additional column labels:

     C7:SOLD TO
     E7:/FR
     /R:F7.G7
     E7:AMOUNT   F7:TAX

We right-justify the amount and tax columns to create a neater form appearance.

The net amount equals the sales price, plus the tax. Thus, using a structured format, we write:

     G7:NET
       G8: +E8+F8
       /R:G9.G29:RR

Next, we use the REPEAT LABEL (/−) command, followed by a dash, to draw a line across the bottom of the form:

     A30:/− −
     /R:B30.G30

Finally, we compute the total sales by summing the sales column:

```
D31:TOTALS
    E31:@SUM(E8.E29)
    /R:F31.G31:RR
```

We will now save the sales register on diskette. We do this by using the STORAGE (/SS) command. We select a file name, SLREG.VC, that will be easy to recall. We then create a disk file by writing:

```
/SS SLREG.VC
```

Note: be sure to save all your spreadsheet instructions on a VisiCalc diskette, as soon as you enter them into your computer.

You may also wish to save your spreadsheets with the entered data. If you do this, however, be sure to use different file names for these spreadsheets, so that your blank spreadsheet will also be saved. For example, if you call the blank sales register SLREG.VC, you might want to call the registers with data SL1REG.VC, SL2REG.VC, etc.

DATA ENTRY

We are now ready to enter the data. Figure 2.4 shows a sample data entry:

```
    A8:"  1/4          B8:1000           C8:BLUE FOX
    D8:100
```

Figure 2.4: Sample Data Entry

In this example, we have specified the date in label format by using the quote symbol. The invoice numbers appear in integer format because we have used the /FL command. (That's right; try it!)

Note that in the printed example in Figure 2.2, a string of 0s appears in the net column—even though there are no calculations evident. This is because the VisiCalc program multiplies the blank entries in columns E and F, and generates a 0 result. This has absolutely no effect—other than an aesthetic one—on the report.

ADDITIONAL REMARKS

As it is currently specified, the sales register has 22 rows of data. If you require more rows for your application, you can add them in one of two ways. If you are adding only a few rows, the simplest way is to use the INSERT ROW (/IR) command. Simply place the cursor anywhere in row 29 and type the /IR command as many times as the number of rows you wish to add. The VisiCalc program will automatically adjust all the formulas.

There is, however, a more general procedure for adding a large number of rows. For example, to add 30 rows to the sales register you would use the following sequence of instructions:

```
A30:/R:A30.F30:A60
/B
/R:B30.F30

D31:/B
/R:E31.F31

D61:TOTALS
  E61:@SUM(E8.E59)
  /R:F61.G61:RR

G8:/R:G9.G59:RR
```

In the above sequence, the first two instructions move the dashed line to row 60; the next two move the totals; and the final instructions recompute the calculations for the net amount. In general, you can use any of these techniques to extend any of the forms described in this book. You may also use the MOVE (/M) command to relocate rows or columns.

Note: If you intend to use this register for a retail business, you may want to make one more modification. You may want to modify the form, so that it automatically computes sales tax. For example, to compute the sales tax at 6.5% you would include the following instructions:

```
F7:TAX
  F8: .065*E8
  /R:F9.F29:R
```

Figure 2.5 shows a sales register with automatic tax calculation.

```
       A          B          C          D          E          F          G
 1                                MYCO INC.
 2                      415 WEST HARRISON STREET
 3                      JACKSON    CALIF.   94223
 4
 5                      SALES      REGISTER                    JAN. 1982
 6    ================================================================
 7    DATE      INVOICE    SOLD TO              AMOUNT      TAX      NET
 8    1/4       1000       BLUE FOX             100.00     6.50    106.50
 9    1/4       1001       OSCARS                75.00     4.88     79.88
10    1/4       1002       DOROS                 60.00     3.90     63.90
11    1/4       1003       ERNIES               125.00     8.13    133.13
12    1/4                  CASH                 351.40    22.84    374.24
13    1/5       1004       BLUE FOX              90.00     5.85     95.85
14    1/5       1005       DOROS                 85.00     5.53     90.53
15    1/5       1006       ERNIES               130.00     8.45    138.45
16    1/5                  CASH                 303.39    19.72    323.11
17    1/6       1007       DOROS                120.00     7.80    127.80
18    1/6       1008       OSCARS                80.00     5.20     85.20
19    1/6       1009       BLUE FOX              70.00     4.55     74.55
20                                                          0.00      0.00
21                                                          0.00      0.00
22                                                          0.00      0.00
23                                                          0.00      0.00
24                                                          0.00      0.00
25                                                          0.00      0.00
26                                                          0.00      0.00
27                                                          0.00      0.00
28                                                          0.00      0.00
29                                                          0.00      0.00
30    ----------------------------------------------------------------
31                        TOTALS             1589.79    103.34   1693.13
```

Figure 2.5: SALES REGISTER With Modifications

CHECK REGISTER

Let's now use the VisiCalc program to design a spreadsheet for recording checks and deposits for a one-month period. We will design this register so that it is useful for both business and personal applications.

APPLICATION EXAMPLE

You want to design a check register that will maintain your checking account information for one month. You plan to record the following information: the check number, the date, a description of the check, the amount of the check, the amount of the deposit, and a running balance. You also want to maintain column totals for the CHECK and DEPOSIT columns.

SPREADSHEET DESIGN

The layout for the check register is very similar to that of the sales register. Figure 2.6 shows a sample layout. An example of a completed check register appears in Figure 2.7.

```
NUMBER     DATE DESCRIPTION      CHECK    DEPOSIT   BALANCE

                 BALANCE FORWARD                    1000.00
100         1/1  ATLAS REALTY    300.00             700.00
```

Figure 2.6: Preliminary Layout: CHECK REGISTER

	A	B	C	D	E	F	G
1				MYCO INC.			
2			415 WEST HARRISON STREET				
3			JACKSON CALIF. 94223				
4							
5			CHECK	REGISTER			JAN. 1982
6	===						
7	NUMBER	DATE	DESCRIPTION		CHECK	DEPOSIT	BALANCE
8			BALANCE	FORWARD			1000.00
9	100	1/1	ATLAS	REALTY	300.00		700.00
10	101	1/1	BAKERY	SUPPLY	176.55		523.45
11	102	1/1	VALLEY	STATIONER	22.19		501.26
12	500	1/3	DEPOSIT			442.19	943.45
13	501	1/4	DEPOSIT			1000.00	1943.45
14	103	1/5	GOLDEN	DAIRY	122.32		1821.13
15	104	1/6	DELTA	LINEN	23.00		1798.13
16	105	1/6	BAKERY	ASSOC	25.00		1773.13
17	106	1/7	CASH		100.00		1673.13
18	501	1/7	DEPOSIT			412.34	2085.47
19	107	1/9	NW GAS		50.25		2035.22
20	108	1/9	PAC ELECTRICITY		44.18		1991.04
21	109	1/9	PAC TELEPHONE		27.79		1963.25
22	110	1/10	HAROLD	SMITH	100.00		1863.25
23	111	1/12	JACKSON	BEE	18.00		1845.25
24	112	1/12	PEGGY	WATSON	175.00		1670.25
25	113	1/12	BAKERY	SUPPLY	55.00		1615.25
26	114	1/15	PELHAM		28.72		1586.53
27							1586.53
28							1586.53
29							1586.53
30	---						
31			TOTALS		1268.00	1854.53	

Figure 2.7: CHECK REGISTER

SPREADSHEET INSTRUCTIONS

Figure 2.8 shows the spreadsheet instructions for this example. Let's examine them in detail.

```
/CY
/SL MASTER.VC
/GF$
    C5:CHECK            D5:REGISTER          G5:JAN. 1982
    A7:/FR NUMBER
      A8:/FI
      /R:A9.A29
B7:" DATE               C7:DESCRIPTI
    D7:ON               E7:/FR CHECK         F7:/FR DEPOSIT
    G7:/FR BALANCE
      G9:+G8+F9—E9
      /R:G10.G29:RRR
A30:/——
/R:B30.H30
C31:TOTALS
    E31:@SUM(E8.E29)
    F31:@SUM(F8.F29)
```

Figure 2.8: Spreadsheet Instructions: CHECK REGISTER

As before, we begin by clearing the screen, loading the master form, specifying the dollar format, and labeling the title. For this example, we want to calculate the balance after the first check. To do this, we use the following formula:

Balance = Balance Forward + Deposit − Check

For the subsequent balances we use the formula:

Balance = Previous Balance + Deposit − Check

The instruction sequence:

```
G7:/FR BALANCE
  G9:+G8+F9—E9
  /R:G10.G29:RRR
```

sets up the required format. The next sequence:

```
C31:TOTALS
    E31:@SUM(E8.E29)
    F31:@SUM(F8.F29)
```

totals the checks and deposits.

DATA ENTRY

Let's now enter the sample data. To do this, we write:

A9: **100**	B9:" **1/1**	C9: **ATLAS**
D9: **REALTY**	E9: **300**	

Note the following:

- To enter the dates as labels we have used the quote symbol. We have also used leading spaces to separate the date from the check number.

- We have placed the item descriptions in a double column, so that we can easily split long words if necessary. Once a coordinate position is filled, we can then simply move the cursor right and continue to type the item description.

In the completed check register in Figure 2.7, if a check or deposit is not entered, the account balance will be duplicated. This is due to the way the VisiCalc program performs its internal arithmetic: as you make an entry, the balance changes.

ADDITIONAL REMARKS

As in the previous example, you can add rows to accommodate additional checks or deposits. The simplest way to do this is by using the INSERT ROW command. Recall that this command automatically keeps all formulas correct.

You may find it most convenient to maintain a separate register for each month. To do this, you first create a blank check register, by using the spreadsheet specification just described, then you use the STORAGE (/SS) command to make twelve copies of the blank register on diskette. Be sure to give each disk file a different name. For example, you could create files for January, February, and March as follows:

```
/SS CKJAN.VC
/SS CKFEB.VC
/SS CKMAR.VC
```

EXPENSE REGISTER

We will now show how data from one display can become a source for another. In this example, we will use data from the check register to allocate expenses automatically. We could allocate the expenses manually; however, it is much easier to use the VisiCalc program to perform the account allocation. We can do this by simply adding an account code to the check information in the check register, and then using the VisiCalc @IF function.

APPLICATION EXAMPLE

Let's assume that you need to keep track of expenses in eleven categories and you want to compute monthly totals. You plan to have the expenses categorized automatically, as you enter information about each check. To do this, you need to add a two-digit expense account code.

SPREADSHEET DESIGN

Figure 2.9 shows a sample layout of an expense register spreadsheet. To record expenses in eleven different categories, we assign one of eleven different account codes to each check; we then use the VisiCalc @IF function to distribute the expenses into their proper columns.

If we store the expense register in the same disk file as the check register, the VisiCalc program will make entries automatically. By carefully aligning the check and expense registers, we can

NUMBER	MATLS 1	SUPPLIES 2	. . .	TAXES 10	INSURANCE 11
100	321.21				
101		98.27			
.					
.					
TOTALS	321.21	98.27		100.00	75.00

Figure 2.9: Preliminary Layout: EXPENSE REGISTER

display check and expense account information in one row. As shown in Figure 2.11, it is best to put the account number below the expense account categories and then align these categories with the row containing the balance forward.

Figure 2.10 shows the check register with the expense account code added. The expense register appears in Figure 2.11.

	A	B	C	D	E	F	G	H
1				MYCO INC.				
2			415 WEST HARRISON STREET					
3			JACKSON CALIF. 94223					
4								
5			CHECK	REGISTER				JAN. 1982
6	===
7	NUMBER	DATE	CODE	DESCRIPTION		CHECK	DEPOSIT	BALANCE
8				BALANCE	FORWARD			1000.00
9	100	1/1	4	ATLAS	REALTY	300.00		700.00
10	101	1/1	1	BAKERY	SUPPLY	176.55		523.45
11	102	1/1	2	VALLEY	STATIONER	22.19		501.26
12	500	1/3		DEPOSIT			442.19	943.45
13	501	1/4		DEPOSIT			1000.00	1943.45
14	103	1/5	1	GOLDEN	DAIRY	122.32		1821.13
15	104	1/6	2	DELTA	LINEN	23.00		1798.13
16	105	1/6	6	BAKERY	ASSOC	25.00		1773.13
17	106	1/7	6	CASH		100.00		1673.13
18	501	1/7		DEPOSIT			412.34	2085.47
19	107	1/9	5	NW GAS		50.25		2035.22
20	108	1/9	5	PAC ELECTRICITY		44.18		1991.04
21	109	1/9	5	PAC TELEPHONE		27.79		1963.25
22	110	1/10	8	HAROLD	SMITH	100.00		1863.25
23	111	1/12	7	JACKSON	BEE	18.00		1845.25
24	112	1/12	3	PEGGY	WATSON	175.00		1670.25
25	113	1/12	1	BAKERY	SUPPLY	55.00		1615.25
26	114	1/15	7	PELHAM		28.72		1586.53
27								1586.53
28								1586.53
29								1586.53
30	---
31				TOTALS		1268.00	1854.53	

Figure 2.10:
First Part of EXPENSE REGISTER (CHECK REGISTER With Expense Account Code)

	I	J	K	L	M	N

					EXPENSE	REGISTER
	NUMBER	MATLS	SUPPLIES	PAYROLL	RENT	UTIL
		1	2	3	4	5
	100	0.00	0.00	0.00	300.00	0.00
	101	176.55	0.00	0.00	0.00	0.00
	102	0.00	22.19	0.00	0.00	0.00
	500	0.00	0.00	0.00	0.00	0.00
	501	0.00	0.00	0.00	0.00	0.00
	103	122.32	0.00	0.00	0.00	0.00
	104	0.00	23.00	0.00	0.00	0.00
	105	0.00	0.00	0.00	0.00	0.00
	106	0.00	0.00	0.00	0.00	0.00
	501	0.00	0.00	0.00	0.00	0.00
	107	0.00	0.00	0.00	0.00	50.25
	108	0.00	0.00	0.00	0.00	44.18
	109	0.00	0.00	0.00	0.00	27.79
	110	0.00	0.00	0.00	0.00	0.00
	111	0.00	0.00	0.00	0.00	0.00
	112	0.00	0.00	175.00	0.00	0.00
	113	55.00	0.00	0.00	0.00	0.00
	114	0.00	0.00	0.00	0.00	0.00
	0	0.00	0.00	0.00	0.00	0.00
	0	0.00	0.00	0.00	0.00	0.00
	0	0.00	0.00	0.00	0.00	0.00
	-------	-------	-------	-------	-------	-------
		353.87	45.19	175.00	300.00	122.22

	O	P	Q	R	S	T

MISC	ADVT	LEGAL	ACCT	TAXES	INS
6	7	8	9	10	11
0.00	0.00	0.00	0.00	0.00	0.00
0.00	0.00	0.00	0.00	0.00	0.00
0.00	0.00	0.00	0.00	0.00	0.00
0.00	0.00	0.00	0.00	0.00	0.00
0.00	0.00	0.00	0.00	0.00	0.00
0.00	0.00	0.00	0.00	0.00	0.00
0.00	0.00	0.00	0.00	0.00	0.00
25.00	0.00	0.00	0.00	0.00	0.00
100.00	0.00	0.00	0.00	0.00	0.00
0.00	0.00	0.00	0.00	0.00	0.00
0.00	0.00	0.00	0.00	0.00	0.00
0.00	0.00	0.00	0.00	0.00	0.00
0.00	0.00	100.00	0.00	0.00	0.00
0.00	18.00	0.00	0.00	0.00	0.00
0.00	0.00	0.00	0.00	0.00	0.00
0.00	0.00	0.00	0.00	0.00	0.00
0.00	28.72	0.00	0.00	0.00	0.00
0.00	0.00	0.00	0.00	0.00	0.00
0.00	0.00	0.00	0.00	0.00	0.00
0.00	0.00	0.00	0.00	0.00	0.00
-------	-------	-------	-------	-------	-------
125.00	46.72	100.00	0.00	0.00	0.00

Figure 2.11: EXPENSE REGISTER

SPREADSHEET INSTRUCTIONS

Figure 2.12 shows the spreadsheet instructions for the expense register. Let's examine them.

```
/CY
/SL CKREG.VC
M5:EXPENSE              N5:REGISTER
C7:/IC
C6:/ — =
/R:D6.T6
   C7:CODE
      C8:/FL
      /R:C9.C29
I7:/FR
/R:J7.T7
   I7:NUMBER
      I9:/FI+A9
      /R:I10.I29:R
   J7:MATLS
      J8:/FI 1
      J9:@IF(C9=J8,F9,0)
      /R:J10.J29:RNR
   K7:SUPPLIES
      K8:/FI 2
      K9:@IF(C9=K8,F9,0)
      /R:K10.K29:RNR
   L7:PAYROLL
      L8:/FI 3
      L9:@IF(C9=L8,F9,0)
      /R:L10.L29:RNR
   M7:RENT
      M8:/FI 4
      M9:@IF(C9=M8,F9,0)
      /R:M10.M29:RNR
```

Figure 2.12: Spreadsheet Instructions: EXPENSE REGISTER (continues)

```
        N7:UTIL
          N8:/FI 5
          N9:@IF(C9=N8,F9,0)
          /R:N10.N29:RNR
        O7:MISC
          O8:/FI 6
          O9:@IF(C9=O8,F9,0)
          /R:O10.O29:RNR
        P7:ADVT
          P8:/FI 7
          P9: @IF(C9=P8,F9,0)
          /R:P10.P29:RNR
        Q7:LEGAL
          Q8:/FI 8
          Q9:@IF(C9=Q8,F9,0)
          /R:Q10.Q29:RNR
        R7:ACCT
          R8:/FI 9
          R9:@IF(C9=R8,F9,0)
          /R:R10.R29:RNR
        S7:TAXES
          S8:/FI 10
          S9:@IF(C9=S8,F9,0)
          /R:S10.S29:RNR
        T7:INS
          T8:/FI 11
          T9:@IF(C9=T8,F9,0)
          /R:T10.T29:RNR
      J31:@SUM(J9.J29)
      /R:K31.T31:RR
```

Figure 2.12: Spreadsheet Instructions: EXPENSE REGISTER (cont.)

We use the STORAGE LOAD (/SL) command to bring the check register spreadsheet from diskette. We then specify the title (for the expense register) and the column headings in the usual way.

To obtain automatic expense allocation, we next add an expense code to each check. To do this, we must add a column to the check register between the check number and the description. The sequence:

```
C7:/IC
C6:/ — =
/R:D6.T6
        C7:CODE
        C8:/FL
        /R:C9.C29
```

sets up the new column. We use the REPEATING LABEL command at C6 because the line that goes across the register was broken when we added the new column. Next, we replicate a left format instruction down the code column.

Finally, we enter the formulas. In addition to entering the formulas we also want to copy the check number from the check register to the expense register. We do this as a convenient reference in case we want to print the register separately. The sequence:

```
I7:NUMBER
    I9:/FI + A9
    /R:I10.I29:R
```

accomplishes this copy operation.

Let's now examine in detail how a check amount is entered in the appropriate expense column. To do this, let's look at a portion of a typical register. (See Figure 2.13.)

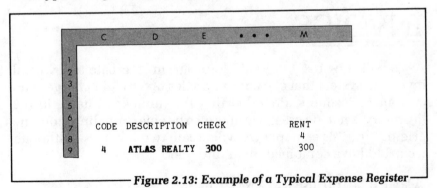

Figure 2.13: Example of a Typical Expense Register

In the register in Figure 2.13, the Atlas Realty check is coded to expense category 4—the category for rent. We can use the "@IF" function in the rent column to transfer the amount of the rent. In

English, we would write this as:

IF CODE = 4, THEN COPY CHECK, OTHERWISE, ENTER 0.

In VisiCalc notation, we specify this as:

M9:@IF(C9=M8,F9,0)

For a typical column, we would enter the formulas:

J7:MATLS

J8:/FI 1

J9:@IF(C9=J8,F9,0)

/R:J10.J29:RNR

The replicate sequence tests each column position, row-by-row, against the constant expense category number.

Finally, to calculate the column totals, we enter the following instruction sequence:

J31:@SUM(J9.J29)

/R:K31.T31:RR

ADDITIONAL REMARKS

Since the expense register in Figure 2.11 is wider than 80 columns you will need to print the expense register in two parts to accommodate standard width printers. To do this, first print the rectangle between coordinates I1 and P31, and then print the data between coordinates Q1 and T31.

INVOICE

We will now use the VisiCalc program to create a powerful invoicing system that can compute sales tax, freight charges and customer discounts. Provided that the number of items in the inventory is not too great, we may also be able to obtain automatic pricing. For this example we will create two invoices—although we could have combined them into one.

APPLICATION EXAMPLE

Let's assume that you want to generate an invoice for a small mail order company in California. Let's *also* assume that on each invoice issued in state, you must include a uniform California sales tax of 6.5%; bills sent out-of-state require no tax. In addition, on each invoice, you must add freight charges based on the total dollar value of the order. These charges are listed in a freight table.

SPREADSHEET DESIGN

Figure 2.14 shows the form layout that we plan to use for this example.

```
    SOLD TO                    CUST CODE
                               ZONE
    ITEM#      DESCRIPTION   QUANT    PRICE      TOTAL
    1234       GLOVES          1      15.95      15.95
                                      TOTAL      15.95
                                      TAX         1.25
                                      FREIGHT     2.35
                                                 -----
                               GRAND  TOTAL      19.55
```

Figure 2.14: Preliminary Layout: INVOICE

To complete this form, we must multiply the quantity purchased, by the unit price, to obtain the total price; we must then add on the individual item totals, to obtain an overall total. Using this total, we must then compute the freight charges. As we will soon see, the freight computation for this example is somewhat complex and, thus, cannot be specified in a single coordinate position as it will lead to a forward reference. If we use this form the way it is designed, we will have a forward reference, which will result in incorrect data. Because the VisiCalc program performs spreadsheet calculations, coordinate-by-coordinate, in either row or column order (as specified by the user), performing a calculation with a coordinate that uses data not yet calculated creates a forward reference. A forward reference results in either the appearance of the symbol @ERROR in the coordinate position or in the computation of incorrect data. (*Note:* The author has taken care to design the spreadsheets in this book so that forward references do not occur.)

Figure 2.15 shows an alternate layout that avoids such problems.

```
     QUANT     PRICE     TOTAL
                         -------------------
                         TOTAL    TAX    FREIGHT
                            GRAND TOTAL
```

Figure 2.15: Alternate Layout: INVOICE

SPREADSHEET INSTRUCTIONS

A sample invoice for this example appears in Figure 2.16. The spreadsheet instructions appear in Figure 2.17. Let's examine these instructions.

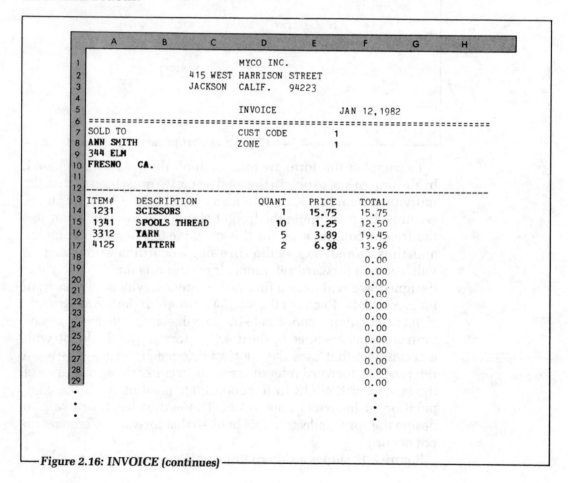

Figure 2.16: INVOICE (continues)

	A	B	C	D	E	F	G	H
30						0.00		
31						=========		
32						TOTAL	TAX	FREIGHT
33						61.66	4.01	1.95
34								
35								
36							GRAND TOT	67.62
37				FREIGHT	TABLE			
38	ZONE1		ZONE2		ZONE3		ZONE4	
39	0.00	1.20	0.00	1.40	0.00	1.50	0.00	1.65
40	10.00	1.40	10.00	1.65	10.00	1.95	10.00	2.20
41	25.00	1.65	25.00	2.10	25.00	2.40	25.00	2.90
42	50.00	1.95	50.00	2.50	50.00	3.00	50.00	3.50
43	100.00	2.40	100.00	2.95	100.00	3.65	100.00	4.25
44								
45								
46				FRT1		1.95		
47				FRT2		0.00		
48				FRT3		0.00		
49				FRT4		0.00		

Figure 2.16: INVOICE (cont.)

```
/CY
/SL MASTER.VC
/GF$
    D5:INVOICE          F5:JAN 12, 19       G5:"82
    A7:SOLD TO          D7:CUST CODE        E7:/FI
    D8:ZONE             E8:/FI
    A12:/ — —
    /R:B12.H12
    A13:ITEM #
     A14:/FL
      /R:A15.A30
    B13:DESCRIPTI       C13:ON
    D13:/FR
    /R:E13.F13
    D13:QUANT
     D14:/FI
      /R:D15.D30
    E13:PRICE
```

Figure 2.17: Spreadsheet Instructions: INVOICE (continues)

```
F13:TOTAL
    F14:+D14*E14
    /R:F15.F30:RR
F31:/−=
F32:/FR
/R:G32.H32
F32:TOTAL
    F33:@SUM(F14.F30)
G32:TAX
    G33: .065*F33*E7
H32:FREIGHT
    H33:@SUM(F46.F49)
        F46:@LOOKUP(F33,A39.A43) *@IF(E8=1,1,0)
        F47:@LOOKUP(F33,C39.C43) *@IF(E8=2,1,0)
        F48:@LOOKUP(F33,E39.E43)  *@IF(E8=3,1,0)
        F49:@LOOKUP(F33,G39.G43)*@IF(E8=4,1,0)
G36:GRAND TOT
    H36:@SUM(F33.H33)
D37:FREIGHT            E37:TABLE
    A38:ZONE1
    A39:0              B39:1.20
    A40:10             B40:1.40
    A41:25             B41:1.65
    A42:50             B42:1.95
    A43:100            B43:2.40
C38:ZONE2
    C39:0              D39:1.40
    C40:10             D40:1.65
    C41:25             D41:2.10
    C42:50             D42:2.50
    C43:100            D43:2.95
E38:ZONE3
    E39:0              F39:1.50
    E40:10             F40:1.95
    E41:25             F41:2.40
```

Figure 2.17: Spreadsheet Instructions: INVOICE (continues)

```
        E42:50              F42:3.00
        E43:100             F43:3.65
     G38:ZONE4
        G39:0               H39:1.65
        G40:10              H40:2.20
        G41:25              H41:2.90
        G42:50              H42:3.50
        G43:100             H43:4.25
     E46:FRT1            E47:FRT2
     E48:FRT3            E49:FRT4
```

Figure 2.17: Spreadsheet Instructions: INVOICE (cont.)

To maintain the item number and the quantity in integer form, we specify:

```
A13:ITEM #
  A14:/FL
  /R:A15.A30
D13:QUANT
  D14:/FI
  /R:D15.D30
```

Next, to obtain a price total, we multiply the unit price by the quantity and then sum the entire column:

```
F13:TOTAL
  F14:+D14*E14
  /R:F15.F30:RR
F32:TOTAL
  F33:@SUM(F14.F30)
```

A simple way to compute the sales tax is to give each California resident the customer code 1, and each non-resident the code 0. We can then compute the tax by multiplying the total of the sale by the customer code. This method ensures that only the Californians pay a tax. We represent this in VisiCalc notation as:

```
G32:TAX
  G33: .065*F33*E7
```

where E7 is the coordinate containing the customer code.

For each zone, we have provided a freight look-up table, categorized by value. We can use the VisiCalc LOOKUP function to obtain the freight charges for each zone. For example, we use the following formula to obtain the freight charge for zone 1:

F46:@LOOKUP(F33,A39.A43)*@IF(E8=1,1,0)

The formula at F46 looks up the total at F33 in the range of A39.A43 and returns a freight value. The @IF function returns a 1 if the customer is in the zone being looked up; otherwise, it returns a 0. The multiplication then assures that the freight charge is either a 0 or the amount looked up. Continuing this process, we find that four freight charges are pulled out, but only one remains non-zero after multiplication by the @IF function. We can then sum these four quantities to obtain the actual freight costs. Thus, we write:

H32:FREIGHT
H33:@SUM(F46.F49)

We store the individual freight charges in F46.F49. Only one of them is non-zero.

ADDITIONAL REMARKS

You can use the INSERT ROW command to include additional rows in this invoice. Because of the large number of formulas used to create this invoice, it is particularly important that you use this command, rather than a more general method.

We previously used the customer code to determine the sales tax. By implementing a few changes, you can modify this form to allow for several different customer discounts. For example, if it is not necessary to compute a tax, you can use the customer code to determine a discount. To do this, you can use the @CHOOSE function (described in the Appendix) to determine the discounts, and then modify the invoice as follows:

G32:DISCOUNT
G33: −F33*@CHOOSE(E7,G46.G49)

The customer codes 1 through 4 reference the stored discounts at coordinates G46 to G49. Let's now complete this example and store discounts of 5, 10, 15 and 20 percent. A reprinted invoice appears in Figure 2.18.

```
        A          B          C          D          E          F          G          H
1                              MYCO INC.
2                        415 WEST HARRISON STREET
3                        JACKSON  CALIF.  94223
4
5                              INVOICE          JAN 12,1982
6 =================================================================
7 SOLD TO                    CUST CODE        1
8 ANN SMITH                  ZONE             1
9 344 ELM
10 FRESNO   CA.
11
12 ----------------------------------------------------------------
13 ITEM#     DESCRIPTION         QUANT     PRICE     TOTAL
14  1231     SCISSORS              1       15.75     15.75
15  1341     SPOOLS THREAD        10        1.25     12.50
16  3312     YARN                  5        3.89     19.45
17  4125     PATTERN               2        6.98     13.96
18                                                    0.00
19                                                    0.00
20                                                    0.00
21                                                    0.00
22                                                    0.00
23                                                    0.00
24                                                    0.00
25                                                    0.00
26                                                    0.00
27                                                    0.00
28                                                    0.00
29                                                    0.00
30                                                    0.00
31                                                 =========
32                                          TOTAL   DISCOUNT  FREIGHT
33                                          61.66    -3.08     1.95
34
35
36                                        GRAND   TOT    60.53
37                        FREIGHT   TABLE
38 ZONE1            ZONE2            ZONE3            ZONE4
39     0.00    1.20      0.00   1.40      0.00   1.50      0.00   1.65
40    10.00    1.40     10.00   1.65     10.00   1.95     10.00   2.20
41    25.00    1.65     25.00   2.10     25.00   2.40     25.00   2.90
42    50.00    1.95     50.00   2.50     50.00   3.00     50.00   3.50
43   100.00    2.40    100.00   2.95    100.00   3.65    100.00   4.25
44
45
46                              FRT1      1.95      .05
47                              FRT2      0.00      .10
48                              FRT3      0.00      .15
49                              FRT4      0.00      .20
```

Figure 2.18: INVOICE SHOWING DISCOUNTS

INCOME STATEMENT

We will now use the VisiCalc program to create a yearly income statement from our monthly expense journal. We can use the standard data exchange method—the Data Interchange Format (DIF)—to exchange data via diskette files, and thus allow one spreadsheet to communicate with another. Using DIF, we can create summary data, such as weekly registers from daily summaries; monthly from weekly; and so forth.

APPLICATION EXAMPLE

You want to use the VisiCalc program to prepare an income statement that will provide a summary of income and expenses for an entire year. You plan to update your statement monthly, with a single sales total that you will enter manually. You plan to obtain your expense figures from the expense register that we designed previously.

SPREADSHEET INSTRUCTIONS

The form layout is quite straightforward. We will not discuss it here. Figure 2.19 shows a sample statement. Figure 2.20 gives the spreadsheet instructions. Let's examine them.

To calculate net income, we subtract returns and allowances from sales. Thus, we write:

```
A13:NET INC
   B13:+B10—B11
   /R:C13.N13:RR
```

The REPLICATE (/R) command repeats this formula for all of the months of the year.

We calculate the total expenses for each month in a similar fashion:

```
A29:TOTAL
   B29:@SUM(B17.B27)
   /R:C29.N29:RR
```

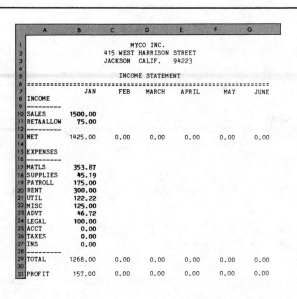

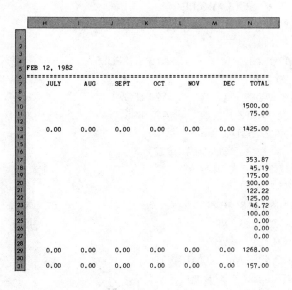

Figure 2.19: INCOME STATEMENT

```
/CY
/SL MASTER.VC
/GF$
    D5:INCOME           E5:STATEMENT        H5:FEB 12,          I5:"1982
    J6:/—=
    /R:L6.N6
    B7:/FR
    /R:C7.N7
    B7:JAN              C7:FEB              D7:MARCH
    E7:APRIL            F7:MAY              G7:JUNE
    H7:JULY             I7:AUG              J7:SEPT
    K7:OCT              L7:NOV              M7:DEC
    A8:INCOME
    A9:/— —
        A10:SALES           A11:RET&ALLOW       A12:/— —
            A13:NET INC
                B13:+B10—B11
                /R:C13.N13:RR
    A15:EXPENSES
    A16:/— —
        A17:MATLS           A18:SUPPLIES        A19:PAYROLL
        A20:RENT            A21:UTIL            A22:MISC
        A23:ADVT            A24:LEGAL           A25:ACCT
        A26:TAXES           A27:INS             A28:/— —
            A29:TOTAL
                B29:@SUM(B17.B27)
                /R:C29.N29:RR
    A31:PROFIT
        B31:+B13—B29
        /R:C31.N31:RR
    N7:TOTAL
        N10:@SUM(B10.M10)
        N11:@SUM(B11.M11)
        N17:@SUM(B17.M17)
        /R:N18.N27:RR
```

Figure 2.20: Spreadsheet Instructions: INCOME STATEMENT

To calculate the profit we use the net income, minus the expenses. Thus, we write:

```
A31:PROFIT
   B31:+B13—B29
   /R:C31.N31:RR
```

In the YTD column we perform the addition horizontally so that we can obtain a summary of each expense category. This is given by:

```
N7:TOTAL
   N10:@SUM(B10.M10)
   N11:@SUM(B11.M11)
   N17:@SUM(B17.M17)
   /R:N18.N27:RR
```

DATA ENTRY

It is now time to enter the data. We will enter the sales data, returns and allowances manually from a monthly journal. We will use the file transfer capability of the VisiCalc program to obtain the expense data from the expense register.

First, we use the STORAGE (/SL) command to load the monthly expense register:

```
/SL EXPREG.VC
```

To set up the VisiCalc screen in the format shown in Figure 2.21, we use the HORIZONTAL TITLES (/TH) command to fix the horizontal labels in place.

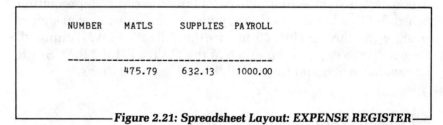

NUMBER	MATLS	SUPPLIES	PAYROLL
------	-----	--------	-------
	475.79	632.13	1000.00

Figure 2.21: Spreadsheet Layout: EXPENSE REGISTER

The total expenses for the month appear in positions J31 through T31. The data depend, of course, on the information previously entered. For each month, we want to transfer the totals in

J31 through T31 to the appropriate monthly expense column of the annual expense summary.

To do this, we create a DIF file for the summarized expenses. We move the cursor to J31 by writing:

```
J31:
```

We then invoke the SAVE command in the DIF by writing:

```
/S#S CKREG.DIF
```

(*Note*: IBM Personal Computer users should omit the DIF extension.) We answer the prompts by moving the cursor to T31 and indicating row order by writing:

```
T31:
R
```

We have now saved the expense data on the diskette in the DIF format. Next, we transfer the data to the annual income summary using the following sequence:

```
/CY
/SL INC.VC
B17:
/S#L CKREG.DIF
C
```

ADDITIONAL REMARKS

It is normally the case that you would not account for all of your expenses on an expense register. For example, depreciation is a non-cash expense that can be obtained from a depreciation schedule. To add information to your expense journal, you simply position the cursor at line 30 and use the INSERT ROW command. Remember to expand the range of the DATA FILE TRANSFER command to account for the additional expense items.

SUMMARY

This chapter has been designed to help you increase your knowledge of the VisiCalc program. It has offered examples and explanations that have demonstrated the use of the VisiCalc program for preparing a sales register, a check register, an expense register, an invoice, and an income statement. This chapter has also demonstrated how you can easily transfer data from one statement to another, and how you can combine information from previous statements. In summary, it has introduced many important features of the VisiCalc program, as well as several useful examples.

FINANCE

*Comparative Income Statement   Comparative Balance Sheet   Key Ratios
Depreciation   Alternative Investment   Capital Equipment Replacement
Lease Purchase Decision   Investment Decision   Project Selection
Discounted Bonds   Portfolio Analysis*

OVERVIEW

In this chapter we will use the VisiCalc program to prepare financial reports. We will create a comparative income statement and a comparative balance sheet, and then use information from these reports to calculate key business ratios.

Next, we will prepare a depreciation schedule. Then, we will set up a spreadsheet to calculate the net present value of various investment alternatives.

Finally, we will use the VisiCalc program to determine the internal rate of return on an investment. Because present versions of the VisiCalc program do not offer an IRR function, we must use an iterative method to obtain this calculation.

The examples in this chapter will incorporate several of the more advanced program features of the VisiCalc program. For example, we will use the NET PRESENT VALUE function to analyze investment alternatives, and the DIF format to transfer files of data from one form to another.

COMPARATIVE INCOME STATEMENT

In the previous chapter, we developed a basic income statement for a small business. We will now use the VisiCalc program to create another income statement—one that will include *both* manual and automatic data entry.

APPLICATION EXAMPLE

Your business is growing rapidly. You want to prepare an income statement to keep track of income and expenses for *three* periods: the previous month, the current month, and year-to-date. On this statement you also want to compute percentages in terms of total sales.

SPREADSHEET INSTRUCTIONS

An example of a comparative income statement appears in Figure 3.1. The spreadsheet instructions appear in Figure 3.2. Let's examine these instructions in detail.

	A	B	C	D	E	F	G	H	I
1				MYCO INC.					
2			415 WEST HARRISON STREET						
3			JACKSON CALIF. 94223						
4									
5			STATEMENT OF OPERATIONS					JUNE 1982	
6	===								
7		MAY	%	YTD	%	JUNE	%	YTD	%
8									
9	NET SALES	101350	100	498145	100	99325	100	597470	100
10	COST	48996	48	247684	50	49062	49	296746	50
11		====...							
12	GR PROFIT	52354	52	250461	50	50263	51	300724	50
13									
14	SALES EXP	18672	18	89156	18	19852	20	109008	18
15	G&A	9967	10	51058	10	10211	10	61269	10
16	INTEREST	7462	7	30145	6	6983	7	37128	6
17		====...							
18		36101		170359		37046		207405	
19	NET BT	16253	16	80102	16	13217	13	93319	16
20									
21	INC TAX	6501	6	32041	6	5287	5	37328	6
22									
23	NET	9752	10	48061	10	7930	8	55991	9

Figure 3.1: A COMPARATIVE INCOME STATEMENT

```
/CY
/SL MASTER.VC
/GFI
C5:STATEMENT        D5:" OF OPERA        E5:TIONS
I6:/−=
H5:JUNE 1982
B7:/FR MAY
A9:NET SALES        A10:COST
B11:/−=
/R:C11.I11
    A12:GR PROFIT
        B12:+B9−B10
A14:SALES EXP       A15:G&A                 A16:INTEREST
    B17:/−=
    /R:C17.I17
    A19:NET BT
        B18:@SUM(B14.B16)
        B19:+B12−B18
A21:INC TAX
    B21:.4*B19
A23:NET
    B23:+B19−B21
C7:/FR "%
    C9:100
    C10:100*B10/B9
    C12:100*B12/B9
    C14:100*B14/B9
    C15:100*B15/B9
    C16:100*B16/B9
    C19:100*B19/B9
    C21:100*B21/B9
    C23:100*B23/B9
D7:/FR YTD
    B9:/R.B23:D9:RRR RRR RRR
E7:/FR "%
```

Figure 3.2: Spreadsheet Instructions:
COMPARATIVE INCOME STATEMENT (continues)

```
    C9:/R.C23:E9:RR RR RR RR RR RR RR RR
F7:/FR JUNE
    B9:/R.B23:F9:RRR RRR RRR
G7:/FR "%
    C9:/R.C23:G9:RR RR RR RR RR RR RR RR
H7:/FR YTD
    H9:+D9+F9
    H10:+D10+F10
    H12:+H9-H10
    H14:+D14+F14
    H15:+D15+F15
    H16:+D16+F16
    H18:@SUM(H14.H16)
    H19:+H12-H18
    H21:+D21+F21
    H23:+D23+F23
I7:/FR "%
    C9:/R.C23:I9:RR RR RR RR RR RR RR RR
```

Figure 3.2:
Spreadsheet Instructions:COMPARATIVE INCOME STATEMENT (cont.)

We begin by entering manually all relevant data pertaining to sales, cost of sales, sales expenses, and general and administrative expenses. Next, we enter the figures for the previous month and year-to-date. (*Note:* we can also obtain these figures automatically from a prior monthly income statement by using a file transfer in the DIF format.)

Next, we calculate the gross profit:

$$\text{Gross Profit} = \text{Net Sales} - \text{Cost of Sales}$$

In VisiCalc notation, we write:

```
A12:GR PROFIT
    B12:+B9-B10
```

Next, we total the expenses:

$$\text{Expense} = \text{Sales Expense} + \text{G\&A} + \text{Interest}$$

In VisiCalc notation, we write:

B18:@SUM(B14.B16)

Then, we subtract the totals of these two coordinates to obtain the pre-tax net:

A19:NET BT
B19:+B12—B18

For this example, we assume a 40% tax rate. Thus, we calculate the income tax by writing:

A21:INC TAX
B21: .4✶B19

Finally, we calculate the bottom line profit by subtracting the income tax from the pre-tax net:

A23:NET
B23:+B19–B21

We calculate the percentages in terms of net sales by dividing each entry by the net sales and multiplying by 100:

Gross Profit % = (Gross Profit)/Sales✶100

In VisiCalc notation, we specify this as:

C12:100✶B12/B9

Next, we replicate the percentages and calculations from the monthly columns into the appropriate columns for calculating the next month's percentages and profits. To replicate the first month into the second month, we write:

B9:/R.B23:D9:RRR RRR RRR

We use similar expressions to replicate the balance of the columns. *Note:* the spaces between the groups of R's appear only for reasons of legibility—they need not be keyed in.

Finally, we update the new year-to-date figures by adding the previous year-to-date total to the current month's entries. For example, to compute the new year-to-date interest, we write:

H16:+D16+F16

ADDITIONAL REMARKS

As we explained earlier, it is not necessary to enter the year-to-date figures by hand—you can use a file transfer in the DIF format to update the file. It is possible to save your updated figures in a DIF file so that you can read them into the next month's income statement by writing:

```
H9:
/S#S      INC.DIF
H23:
C
```

You can easily modify a spreadsheet to meet your specific needs. For example, you can use the INSERT ROW feature of VisiCalc to add a row, or you can use the INSERT COLUMN command to add a column. This makes it easier to examine and compare actual and budgeted income statement items.

Be sure to save this spreadsheet on diskette, so that we can use it with the next two examples.

COMPARATIVE BALANCE SHEET

We will now develop a balance sheet that is similar to the income statement we have just designed. We will enter the data manually; the VisiCalc program will calculate the percentages— thus reducing the overall effort required to produce a completed balance sheet. Once we have developed the balance sheet, we will combine it with information from our income statement to determine key financial ratios.

APPLICATION EXAMPLE

Let's assume that you need to create a balance sheet for your company that will track assets and liabilities and provide totals and percentages for a two-month period. You also want to compute increases and decreases in the various balance sheet items.

SPREADSHEET INSTRUCTIONS

Figure 3.3 shows a printout of a completed balance sheet. The spreadsheet instructions for this statement appear in Figure 3.4. We will store the balance sheet on the same diskette file as the income statement, so that we can more easily calculate the key ratios. Let's now examine the spreadsheet instructions in detail.

	A	B	C	D	E	F	G
24			COMPARATIVE	BALANCE	SHEET		
25			MAY	%	JUNE	%	CHANGE
26	ASSETS						
27	CASH & EQUIVALENTS		234794	21	238812	22	4018
28	ACCOUNTS RCVBL		122700	11	124442	11	1742
29	INVENTORY		256379	23	254933	23	-1446
30	PREPAID EXPENSE		52341	5	53818	5	1477
31			---				
32			666214		672005		5791
33	INVESTMENTS		50000	5	50000	5	0
34							
35	LAND		50000	5	50000	5	0
36	BUILDINGS		275634	25	275634	25	0
37	EQUIPMENT		365893	33	365893	33	0
38			---				
39	LESS DEPRECIATION		300134		303178		
40			---				
41			391393		388349		
42	TOTAL ASSETS		1107607	100	1110354	100	2747
43							
44	LIABILITIES						
45	NOTES PAYABLE		15000	1	15000	1	0
46	ACCOUNTS PAYABLE		185777	17	188635	17	2858
47	ACCRUED TAXES		43222	4	47823	4	4601
48	ACCRUED EXPENSES		39845	4	37812	3	-2033
49			---				
50			283844	26	289270	26	5426
51	LONG TERM DEBT		275000	25	275000	25	0
52							
53	TOTAL LIABILITIES		558844	50	564270	51	5434
54							
55	OWNERS EQUITY		548763	50	546084	49	-2679
56							
57	LIAB + EQUITY		1107607	100	1110354	100	2747

Figure 3.3: A COMPARATIVE BALANCE SHEET

```
/CY
/SL INC2.VC
C24:" COMPARAT        D24:IVE BALAN        E24:CE SHEET
    C25:/FR MAY
    A26:ASSETS
        A27:CASH & EQ        B27:UIVALENT
        A28:ACCOUNTS        B28:RCVBL
        A29:INVENTORY
        A30:PREPAID        B30:EXPENSE
    C31:/— —
    /R:D31.G31
        C32:@SUM(C26.C30)
        A33:INVESTMEN        B33:TS
        A35:LAND        A36:BUILDINGS        A37:EQUIPMENT
    C38:/— —
    /R:D38.G38
        A39:LESS DEPR        B39:ECIATION
    C40:/— —
    /R:D40.G40
    C41:@SUM(C35.C37)—C39
        A42:TOTAL ASS        B42:ETS
        C42:+C32+C33+C41
        A44:LIABILITI        B44:ES
            A45:NOTES PAY        B45:ABLE
            A46:ACCOUNTS        B46:PAYABLE
            A47:ACCRUED        B47:TAXES
            A48:ACCRUED        B48:EXPENSES
            C49:/— —
            /R:D49.G49
            C50:@SUM(C44.C48)
            A51:LONG TERM        B51:" DEBT
            A53:TOTAL LIA        B52:BILITIES
            C53:@SUM(C50.C51)
            A55:OWNERS EQ        B55:UITY
            C55:+C42—C53
```

Figure 3.4: Spreadsheet Instructions: COMPARATIVE BALANCE SHEET (continues)

```
        A57:LIAB +              B57:EQUITY
          C57:+C53+C55
      D25:/FR "%
          D27:100*C27/C42
          /R:D28.D30:RN
          D33:100*C33/C42
          /R:D35.D37:RN
          D45:100*C45/C57
          /R:D46.D48:RN
          /R:D50.D51:RN
          D42:100              D53:100*C53/C57
          D55:100*C55/C57
      E25:/FR JUNE
          C27:/R.C57:E27:RR RRR RRR RR RR RR RR
      F25:/FR "%
          D27:/R.D57:F27:RRRRR RRRRR RRRRR RRRRR RRRRR RR RRRR
      G25:/FR CHANGE
          G27:+E27-C27
          /R:G28.G30:RR
          G32:+E32-C32
          G33:+E33-C33
          /R:G35.G37:RR
          G42:+E42-C42
          /R:G45.G48:RR
          /R:G50.G53:RR
          G55:+E55-C55
          G57:+E57-C57
```

Figure 3.4:

Spreadsheet Instructions: COMPARATIVE BALANCE SHEET (cont.)

To load the income statement, we first clear the screen and load the disk file:

```
/CY
/SL INC2.VC
```

(*Note:* We assume here that we have stored the income statement as a disk file named INC2.VC.)

The specification for the balance sheet items is quite straightforward. Due to the long names of the entries we provide two columns for them. Here are the formulas we enter. To compute current assets, we write:

C32:@SUM(C26.C30)

To calculate fixed assets less depreciation, we write:

C41:@SUM(C35.C37)−C39

To compute total assets, in VisiCalc notation, we write:

C42:+C32+C33+C41

To specify current liabilities, we write:

C50:@SUM(C44.C48)

To determine total liabilities, we write:

C53:@SUM(C50.C51)

Next, we replicate the items in the column for May into the column for June by writing:

C27:/R.C57:E27:RR RRR RRR RR RR RR RR

Next, we calculate percentages by dividing each balance sheet item by the total for assets or liabilities, and then multiplying the quotient by 100. For example, to find CASH percentages, we write:

D27:100∗C27/C42

We calculate the change in balance sheet items by subtracting, for each item, the May entry from the June entry.

KEY
RATIOS

To compare the financial health of a company to that of its competition, it is useful to analyze key financial ratios. In this example, we will use information from the income statement and balance sheet to develop these ratios.

APPLICATION EXAMPLE

For your company, you want to calculate the following ratios:

- Return on Assets (ROA)
- Return on Investment (ROI)
- Income to Sales
- Current Ratio
- Quick Ratio
- Debt to Assets
- Collection Period
- Inventory Turnover

SPREADSHEET INSTRUCTIONS

A sample analysis appears in Figure 3.5. The spreadsheet instructions appear in Figure 3.6. For easy access to balance sheet and income statement items, we have stored all three spreadsheets on the same disk file.

	L	M	N	O	P	Q
			KEY RATIOS			
			MAY		JUNE	
ROA			0.11		0.09	
ROI			0.21		0.17	
INC/SALES			0.10		0.08	
CURRENT RATIO			2.35		2.32	
QUICK RATIO			1.44		1.44	
DEBT TO ASSETS			0.25		0.25	
DAYS RECEIVEABLE			36		38	
INVENTORY TURNOVER			5		5	

Figure 3.5: KEY RATIO REPORT

```
/CY
/SL INC2.VC
O5:KEY RATIO          P5:S
N7:/FR MAY            P7:/FR JUNE
N8:/F$
/R:N9.N19
P8:/F$
/R:P9.P19
   L9:ROA
      N9:+B23/C57*12        P9:F23/E57*12
   L11:ROI
      N11:+B23/C55*12     P11:+F23/E55*12
   L13:INC/SALES
      N13:+B23/B9          P13:+F23/F9
   L15:CURRENT       M15:RATIO
      N15:+C32/C50         P15:+E32/E50
   L17:QUICK         M17:RATIO
      N17:(C32−C29)/C50 P17:(E32−E29)/E50
   L19:DEBT/ASSE     M19:TS
      N19:+C51/C42         P17+E51/E42
   L21:DAYS RECE     M21:IVEABLE
      N21:+C28/(B9/30)  P21:+E28/(F9/30)
   L23:INVENTORY     M23:" TURNOVER
      N23:+B9/C29*12     P23:+F9/E29*12
```

Figure 3.6: Spreadsheet Instructions: KEY RATIOS

We compute the ratios by taking the monthly and year-to-date figures from the appropriate positions on the spreadsheet. Here are the formulas that we will use to make the calculations:

We calculate return on assets as:

(Net Profit after Tax)/(Total Assets)

In VisiCalc notation, we write:

```
L9:ROA
   N9:+B23/C57*12
```

We compute return on investment as:

(Net Profit after Tax)/(Net Worth)

In VisiCalc notation, we write:

L11:ROI

N11:+B23/C55*12

We determine the income to sales ratio:

(Net Profit after Tax)/Sales

by writing:

L13:INC/SALES

N13:+B23/B9

The current ratio is:

(Current Assets)/(Current Liabilities)

In VisiCalc notation, we write:

L15:CURRENT   M15:RATIO

N15:+C32/C50

The quick ratio is:

(Current Assets − Inventory)/Current Liabilities)

In VisiCalc notation, we write:

L17:QUICK   M17:RATIO

N17:(C32−C29)/C50

We specify debt to assets as:

(Total Debt)/(Total Assets)

In VisiCalc notation, we write:

L19:DEBT/ASSE   M19:TS

N19:+C51/C42

The collection period is:

Receivables/(Sales per Day)

In VisiCalc notation, we write:

L21:DAYS RECE   M21:IVEABLE

N21:+C28/(B9/30)

The inventory turnover is defined as:

Sales/Inventory

We write:

L23:INVENTORY   M23:" TURNOVER
    N23:+B9/C29*12

ADDITIONAL REMARKS

It is possible to compute additional ratios of interest by simply using extensions of the methods we have developed in this example. Note that we have specified an income statement, a balance sheet, and a key ratio analysis (together) in one spreadsheet. You could, however, alternately keep them in three separate disk files and simply transfer the necessary data using the DIF file transfer method.

DEPRECIATION

We will now use the VisiCalc program to set up a depreciation schedule. In order to explore various depreciation methods we will use several methods for depreciating different assets. We will use the same initial asset value, salvage value, and life, to show the effects of the different methods.

APPLICATION EXAMPLES

You want to establish a depreciation schedule for your company. You set the asset value, salvage value, and life as the initial parameters. For any asset, you can apply the straight line, the double declining balance, and the sum of the year's digits method, as desired. You want your spreadsheet to show the initial value, the salvage value, the yearly depreciation, and the current value of the asset.

SPREADSHEET INSTRUCTIONS

A sample depreciation schedule appears in Figure 3.7. Figure 3.8 shows the spreadsheet instructions that produced the output in Figure 3.7.

```
         A      B       C       D       E      F      G
1                          MYCO INC.
2                  415 WEST HARRISON STREET
3                  JACKSON  CALIF.   94223
4
5                  DEPRECIATION SCHEDULE        JAN. 1982
6  ==================================================================
7                     ASSET1   ASSET2   ASSET3
8
9  INITIAL  VALUE     20000    20000    20000
10 PRESENT  VALUE     20000    20000    20000
11 LIFE                  8        8        8
12 SALVAGE  VALUE     1000     1000     1000
13 METHOD           ST LINE    DBB   SUM DIGIT
14
15 YEAR                  1        1        1
16 DEPREC            2375     5000     4222
17 END VAL          17625    15000    15778
18
19 YEAR                  2        2        2
20 DEP               2375     3750     3694
21 END VALUE        15250    11250    12083
22
23 YEAR                  3        3        3
24 DEP               2375     2813     3167
25 END VALUE        12875     8438     8917
26
27 YEAR                  4        4        4
28 DEP               2375     2109     2639
29 END VALUE        10500     6328     6278
30
31 YEAR                  5        5        5
32 DEP               2375     1582     2111
33 END VALUE         8125     4746     4167
34
35 YEAR                  6        6        6
36 DEP               2375     1187     1583
37 END VALUE         5750     3560     2583
```

Figure 3.7: A DEPRECIATION SCHEDULE

```
/CY
/GFI
/SL MASTER.VC
C5:DEPRECIAT        D5:ION SCHED        E5:ULE              G5:JAN. 1982
   C7:/FR ASSET1    D7:/FR ASSET2       E7:/FR ASSET3
   A9:INITIAL       B9:VALUE
   A10:PRESENT      B10:VALUE
   A11:LIFE
```

Figure 3.8: Spreadsheet Instructions: DEPRECIATION SCHEDULE (continues)

```
    A12:SALVAGE        B12:VALUE
    A13:METHOD
    A15:YEAR           C15:1          D15:1          E15:1
    A16:DEPREC
       C13:/FR ST LINE
          C16:(C9−C12)/C11
       D13:/FR'' DBB
          D16:+D10/D11*2
       E13:/FR SUM DIGIT
          E16:(E9−E12)*((E11+1−E15)/((E11*(E11+1))/2)
    A17:END VAL
       C17:+C10−C16
       /R:D17.E17:RR
    A19:YEAR
       C19:1+C15
       /R:D19.E19:R
    A20:DEP
       C20:+C16
       D20:+D17/D11*2
       E20:(E9−E12)*((E11+1−E19)/((E11*(E11+1))/2)
    A21:END VALUE
       C21:+C17−C20
       /R:D21.E21:RR
    A19:/R.E19:A23:RRR
    /R.E19:A27:RRR
    /R.E19:A31:RRR
    /R.E19:A35:RRR
    A20:/R.E20:A24:NRN NNN RNN
    /R.E20:A28:NRN NNN RNN
    /R.E20:A32:NRN NNN RNN
    /R.E20:A36:NRN NNN RNN
    A21:/R.E21:A25:RRR RRR
    /R.E21:A29:RRR RRR
    /R.E21:A33:RRR RRR
    /R.E21:A37:RRR RRR
```

Figure 3.8: Spreadsheet Instructions: DEPRECIATION SCHEDULE (cont.)

Asset 1 is to be depreciated by using the straight line method. To calculate the yearly depreciation, we use the following formula:

Depreciation = (Initial Value — Salvage)/Life

In VisiCalc notation, we write:

    C13:/FR ST LINE
     C16:(C9−C12)/C11

The double declining balance method ignores the salvage value of an asset. The first-year depreciation is calculated and then doubled. With the double declining balance method we find depreciation figures by taking the present value, depreciating it over the remaining life, and then doubling the calculated value. We specify this in VisiCalc notation as:

    D13:/FR″   DBB
     D16:+D10/D11∗2

The sum of the year's digits method works as follows. If N is the life of an asset, the sum of the digits is represented as:

    SUM = N∗(N + 1)/2

We calculate depreciation by multiplying the depreciable cost by the number of years remaining, and then dividing the result by the sum of the year's digits. The calculation for the first year is:

    E13:/FR SUM DIGIT
     E16:(E9−E12)∗(E11+1−E15)/((E11∗(E11+1))/2)

For each method the value of the asset at the end of the period is the initial value, less the amount of the depreciation. We enter this formula in all three columns as follows:

    A17:END VAL
     C17:+C10−C16
     /R:D17.E17:RR

For the second year we calculate the depreciation again for each of the three methods. The straight line formula is identical to the formula in C16. We write the formulas for the double declining balance and the sum of the year's digits method as:

    A20:DEP
     D20:+D17/D11∗2
     E20:(E9−E12)∗(E11+1−E19)/((E11∗(E11+1))/2)

Rather than repeat these formulas for each year, we use a series of REPLICATE commands, as shown in the spreadsheet instructions. (See Appendix A for further information on the REPLICATE command.)

ADDITIONAL REMARKS

You may extend this form to track any number of assets by simply adding a new column (by providing a description of the new asset in the parameter table) and then replicating the formulas from the column that contains the desired depreciation method.

ALTERNATIVE INVESTMENT

Many investment examples involve a stream of uneven cash flows. To select the best project from several alternatives we must discount the projected future cash flow to the present, and then select the project or projects with the highest present value. The VisiCalc program provides a built-in NET PRESENT VALUE (@NPV) function that is useful for designing spreadsheets that perform present value analyses.

APPLICATION EXAMPLE

Let's assume that you are considering two investments. Here are the projected cash flows for each investment:

YEAR	INVESTMENT	
	1	2
1	10000	1000
2	11000	10000
3	12000	15000
4	12000	20000
5	12000	20000

You require a 15% return on your funds. You wish to calculate the net present values for each cash flow stream.

SPREADSHEET INSTRUCTIONS

With the NET PRESENT VALUE function we can easily analyze alternative investments. For example, we can use the NET PRESENT VALUE function to determine what might happen if discount rates, down payments, or cash flows are altered. When designing a spreadsheet it is useful to put these parameters, which are likely to vary, in a parameter table; then we can easily make changes and readily see their effects.

The output for this example (shown in Figure 3.9) illustrates the above principles. Figure 3.10 shows the spreadsheet instructions. We have entered free text in this example to make the output more comprehensible.

The layout of the report allows the easy extension of the cash flows to any number of periods. We have positioned the interest rate so that it can be easily changed.

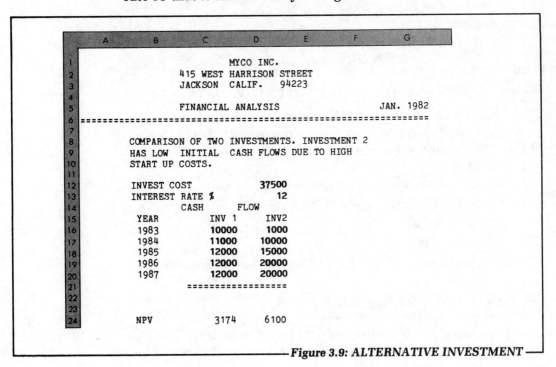

Figure 3.9: ALTERNATIVE INVESTMENT

```
/CY
/SL MASTER.VC
/GFI
C5:FINANCIAL          D5:" ANALYSIS          G5:JAN. 1982
B8:COMPARISO          C8:N OF TWO            D8:INVESTMEN
E8:TS. INVES          F8:TMENT 2             B9:HAS LOW
C9:INITIAL            D9:CASH FLOW           E9:S DUE TO
F9:HIGH               B10:START UP           C10:COSTS.
B12:INVEST            C12:COST
B13:INTEREST          C13:RATE %
C14:CASH              D14:FLOW
B15:YEAR              C15:/FR INV 1          D15:/FR INV 2
B16:1983
B17:1984
B18:1985
B19:1986
B20:1987
C21:/—=               D21:/—=
B24:NPV
    C24:—D12+@NPV(D13/100,C16.C20)
    D24:—D12+@NPV(D13/100,D16.D20)
```

Figure 3.10: Spreadsheet Instructions: ALTERNATIVE INVESTMENT

In this example, we use the @NPV function to compute the net present value of each cash flow. Since the project cost is located at D12 and the interest is at D13, the NPV becomes:

```
B24:NPV
    C24:—D12+@NPV(D13/100,C16.C20)
```

As shown in the output, the two NPVs are:

NPV1 = 3174

NPV2 = 6100

Thus, we would choose investment 2 since it has the higher NPV.

ADDITIONAL REMARKS

This example has been designed to be quite simple. You can easily extend it to account for additional investment alternatives.

To demonstrate the full flexibility and power of the VisiCalc program, you can include more variables in the analysis. We do this in future examples in this book.

CAPITAL EQUIPMENT REPLACEMENT

We will now use the VisiCalc program to create a spreadsheet that can be used for determining whether or not a piece of capital equipment should be replaced. As in the previous example we will compare the net present value of streams of cash flows; however, in this example we will evaluate the cash flows and their sources in more detail.

APPLICATION EXAMPLE

Let's assume that you work for a small manufacturing firm that is considering replacement of a fully-depreciated piece of capital equipment. The company's projected yearly sales are:

1982	100000
1983	105000
1984	110000
1985	114000

You expect that the new piece of equipment will reduce sales costs from sixty to fifty percent. The manufacturer's tax rate is forty percent. The manufacturer requires a return of fifteen percent on invested funds. The new machinery costs $30,000 and has an expected life of four years.

SPREADSHEET INSTRUCTIONS

A sample display of a completed report appears in Figure 3.11. The spreadsheet instructions for this analysis appear in Figure 3.12. Figure 3.11 shows two projected income statements: one with the new machine and one without it. We have used the format that we developed in Chapter 2 to produce this statement. Let's now examine the instructions.

```
         A          B          C          D          E          F          G
1                              MYCO INC.
2                       415 WEST HARRISON STREET
3                       JACKSON  CALIF.  94223
4
5                       EQUIPMENT REPLACEMENT ANALYSIS       JAN. 1982
6   =================================================================
7                  PROJECTED INCOME  CURRENT  MACHINE
8
9                   1982       1983       1984       1985
10  SALES         100000     105000     110000     114000
11  COST           60000      63000      66000      68400
12
13  GP             40000      42000      44000      45600
14
15  SALES&G&A      10000      10500      11000      11400
16  DEPR
17
18  NET BT         30000      31500      33000      34200
19
20  TAX            12000      12600      13200      13680
21
22  NET            18000      18900      19800      20520
23
24                 PROJECTED WITH NEW MACHINE
25
26                  1982       1983       1984       1985
27
28  SALES         100000     105000     110000     114000
29  COST           50000      52500      55000      57000
30
31  GP             50000      52500      55000      57000
32
33  SALES&G&A      10000      10500      11000      11400
34  DEPR            7500       7500       7500       7500
35
36  NET BT         32500      34500      36500      38100
37
38  TAX            13000      13800      14600      15240
39
40  NET            19500      20700      21900      22860
41
42  BENEFIT
43  CHNG INC        1500       1800       2100       2340
44  CHNG DEP        7500       7500       7500       7500
45  TOTAL           9000       9300       9600       9840
46
47  NPV            -3203
```

Figure 3.11: CAPITAL EQUIPMENT REPLACEMENT

```
/CY
/SL MASTER.VC
/GOR
C5:EQUIPMENT        D5:" REPLACEM      E5:ENT ANALY      F5:SIS
G5:JAN. 1982
B7:PROJECTED        C7:" INCOME        D7:CURRENT        E7:MACHINE
B24:PROJECTED       C24:" WITH NEW     D24:" MACHINE
    B9:1982         C9:1983            D9:1984           E9:1985
    B9:/R.E9:B26
    A10:SALES
    A28:SALES
       B28:+B10
       /R:C28.E28:R
    A11:COST
       B11: .6*B10
       /R:C11.E11:R
    A29:COST
       B29: .5*B28
       /R:C29.E29:R
    A13:GP
       B13:+B10−B11
       /R:C13.E13:RR
       A13:/R.E13:A31:RR RR RR RR
    A15:SALES&G&A
       B15: .1*B10
       /R:C15.E15:R
       A15:/R.E15:A33:RRRR
    A16:DEPR
    A34:DEPR
       C34:+B34
       /R:D34.E34:N
    A18:NET BT
       B18:+B13−B15−B16
       /R:C18.E18:RRR
       A18:/R.E18:A36:RRR RRR RRR RRR
```

Figure 3.12: Spreadsheet Instructions: CAPITAL EQUIPMENT REPLACEMENT (continues)

```
A20:TAX
   B20: .4*B18
   /R:C20.E20:R
   A20:/R.E20:A38:RRRR
A22:NET
   B22:+B18-B20
   /R:C22.E22:RR
   A22:/R.E22:A40:RR RR RR RR
A42:BENEFIT
   A43:CHNG INC
      B43:+B40-B22
      /R:C43.E43:RR
   A44:CHNG DEP
      B44:+B34-B16
      /R:C44.E44:RR
   A45:TOTAL
      B45:+B43+B44
      /R:C45.E45:RR
   A47:NPV
      B47:-30000+@NPV(.15,B45.E45)
```

Figure 3.12:
Spreadsheet Instructions: CAPITAL EQUIPMENT REPLACEMENT (cont.)

For this example, we obtain the sales figures from the manufacturer's projections and we calculate the cost of sales from the stated percentages. For the old machine, we use the following calculations:

Cost of Sales = .6*Sales
Gross Profit = Sales − Cost of Sales

In VisiCalc notation, we express this as:

```
A11:COST
   B11: .6*B10
   /R:C11.E11:R
A13:GP
   B13:+B10-B11
   /R:C13.E13:RR
   A13:/R.E13:A31:RR RR RR RR
```

These formulas calculate the cost and gross profit. We replicate these items in both projected income statements.

Similarly, we calculate the other expense items:

Sales & G&A = .1*Sales

In VisiCalc notation, we write:

B15: .1*B10
/R:C15.E15:R

The net profit before tax is:

Net BT = Gross − Sales & G&A − Depr

In VisiCalc notation, we write:

A18:NET BT
B18: +B13−B15−B16
/R:C18.E18:RRR

To determine the tax:

Tax = .4*Net BT

we write:

A20:TAX
B20: .4*B18
/R:C20.E20:R

To specify net income:

Net = Net BT − Tax

in VisiCalc notation, we write:

A22:NET
B22:B18−B20
/R:C22.E22:RR

Again, we replicate these items in both statements.

To determine the benefits of the new machine, we must determine the change in income. To calculate the change

Change = Inc1 − Inc2

we write:

A43:CHNG INC
B43: +B40−B22
/R:C43.E43:RR

Since depreciation is a non-cash expense, we add the change in depreciation to the change in income, to obtain the total cash flow. Thus, we write:

```
A44:CHNG DEP
    B44:+B34—B16
    /R:C44.E44:RR
A45:TOTAL
    B45:+B43+B44
    /R:C45.E45:RR
```

Next, we calculate the net present value by writing:

```
A47:NPV
    B47:—30000+@NPV(.15,B45.E45)
```

As illustrated on the printout, the net present value of the savings is —$3,203. Since this figure is negative it would not be wise to make the replacement.

LEASE PURCHASE DECISION

Following the same procedure used in the last two examples we will now use the VisiCalc program to analyze a lease/purchase situation. Once again, we will use the net present value method to determine which of two cash flows is the more favorable.

APPLICATION EXAMPLE

Your company is considering acquiring a new computerized billing system in order to automate the billing department. You have the option of either purchasing the system for $80,000 or leasing it for $2,000 per month. Computer life is estimated at five years. Your company's sales are $2,000,000 per year and the pre-tax profit is 30%. The company is in the 40% tax bracket and expects a 14% return on invested capital. A previous in-depth study has shown that the new system will reduce billing costs by $3,000 per month.

SPREADSHEET INSTRUCTIONS

A sample display showing the lease purchase figures appears in Figure 3.13. The spreadsheet instructions for this example appear in Figure 3.14.

```
              A         B         C         D         E         F         G
 1                          MYCO INC.
 2                   415 WEST HARRISON STREET
 3                   JACKSON  CALIF.   94223
 4
 5                   LEASE PURCHASE STUDY              FEB. 1982
 6  =================================================================
 7                   1982      1983      1984      1985      1986
 8  PRESENT
 9  ---------
10  SALES        2000000   2100000   2210000   2260000   2310000
11
12  NET BT        600000    630000    663000    678000    693000
13  TAX           240000    252000    265200    271200    277200
14
15  NET           360000    378000    397800    406800    415800
16
17  PURCHASE
18  ---------
19  NET           600000    630000    663000    678000    693000
20  SAL CHNG      -36000    -36000    -36000    -36000    -36000
21  DEPR           16000     16000     16000     16000     16000
22
23  NET BT        620000    650000    683000    698000    713000
24  TAX           248000    260000    273200    279200    285200
25  NET           372000    390000    409800    418800    427800
26
27
28  CASH FLOW      28000     28000     28000     28000     28000
29  NPV            16126
30
31  LEASE
32  ---------
33  NET           600000    630000    663000    678000    693000
34  SAL CHNG      -36000    -36000    -36000    -36000    -36000
35  LEASE          24000     24000     24000     24000     24000
36
37  NET BT        612000    642000    675000    690000    705000
38  TAX           244800    256800    270000    276000    282000
39
40  NET           367200    385200    405000    414000    423000
41
42  CASH FLOW       7200      7200      7200      7200      7200
43  NPV            24718
```

Figure 3.13: LEASE PURCHASE STUDY

/CY
/SL MASTER.VC
/GOR
C5:LEASE PUR   D5:CHASE STU   E5:DY
G5:FEB. 1982
B7:1982   C7:1983   D7:1984   E7:1985
F7:1986
  A8:PRESENT
  A9:/ — —
  A10:SALES
  A12:NET BT
    B12: .3*B10
    /R:C12.F12:R
  A13:TAX
    B13:.4*B12
    /R:C13.F13:R
  A15:NET
    B15:+B12−B13
    /R:C15.F15:RR
  A17:PURCHASE
  A18:/ — —
  A19:NET
    B19:+B12
    /R:C19.F19:R
  A20:SAL CHNG
    B20:−36000
    /R:C20.F20
  A21:DEPR
    B21:16000
    /R:C21.F21
  A23:NET BT
    B23:+B19−B20−B21
    /R:C23.F23:RRR
  A24:TAX

Figure 3.14: Spreadsheet Instructions: LEASE PURCHASE STUDY (continues)

```
        B24: .4*B23
        /R:C24.F24:R
A25:NET
        B25: +B23−B24
        /R:C25.F25:RR
A28:CASH FLOW
        B28: +B25+B21−B15
        /R:C28.F28:RRRR
A29:NPV
        B29: −80000+@NPV(.14,B28.F28)
A31:LEASE
A32:/−−
A33:NET
        B33: +B12
        /R:C33.F33:R
A34:SAL CHNG
        B34: +B20
        /R:C34.F34:R
A35:LEASE
        B35:/R:C35.F35
A37:NET BT
        B37: +B33−B34−B35
        /R:C37.F37:RRR
A38:TAX
        B38: .4*B37
        /R:C38.F38:R
A40:NET
        B40: +B37−B38
        /R:C40.F40:RR
A42:CASH FLOW
        B42: +B40−B15
        /R:C42.F42:RR
A43:NPV
        B43:@NPV (.14,B42.F42)
```

Figure 3.14: Spreadsheet Instructions: LEASE PURCHASE STUDY (cont.)

In this example, we start with a summary income statement for current operations. We assume a modest sales growth. To obtain the expense item figures, we write:

```
A12:NET BT
    B12: .3*B10
    /R:C12.F12:R
A13:TAX
    B13: .4*B12
    /R:C13.F13:R
```

Next, we calculate the net after-tax profit by subtracting the previous totals:

```
A15:NET
    B15: +B12−B13
    /R:C15.F15:RR
```

Under the purchase and lease models we start with a net income that is equal to the present net before taxes. We then compute the new net income and proceed as above.

After the purchase, salaries will change by $3,000 per month. Thus, we enter −$36,000 as the yearly salary change:

```
A20:SAL CHNG
    B20: −36000
    /R:C20.F20
```

Depreciation is one-fifth of the purchase price per year. Thus, we write:

```
A21:DEPR
    B21:16000
    /R:C21.F21
```

The net profit before tax is increased by the salary change and reduced by the depreciation. We express this as:

```
A23:NET BT
    B23: +B19−B20−B21
    /R:C23.F23:RRR
```

Next, we compute the income tax and subtract it from the

before-tax net to obtain the bottom line profit:

    A24:TAX
      B24: .4*B23
      /R:C24.F24:R
    A25:NET
      B25:+B23−B24
      /R:C25.F25:RR

After calculating the tax we must compute the change in net profit and add the depreciation to arrive at the cash flow. We treat the purchase price as a negative cash flow in the first year. We write:

    A28:CASH FLOW
      B28:+B25+B21−B15
      /R:C28.F28:RRRR

The net present value of the purchase price and cash flow are then:

    A29:NPV
      B29:−80000+@NPV(.14,B28.F28)

We evaluate the lease model in a similar way by adjusting the net profit by the salary change and lease price. We have entered the salary change at B34 and the lease at B35; therefore, we write:

    A37:NET BT
      B37:+B33−B34−B35
      /R:C37.F37:RRR

Next, we calculate the new income tax and the resultant cash flow by writing:

    A42:CASH FLOW
      B42:+B40−B15
      /R:C42.F42:RR

Finally, after we replicate the various formulas we compute the net present value by writing:

    A43:NPV
      B43:@NPV(.14,B42.F42)

After reviewing the spreadsheet for both alternatives we see that purchasing the equipment has a higher net present value. For this reason it is the appropriate decision.

INVESTMENT DECISION

We will now review an investment decision using the internal rate of return (IRR). The IRR is the interest rate that equates the present value of future cash flows to the initial cash outlay. Because the VisiCalc program does not have a built-in IRR function, we will use the @NPV function to determine the IRR. We can do this in the following steps:

1. First, we set up a net present value calculation based on after-tax cash flows. We make an educated guess at the interest rate.

2. Then, we subtract the initial cash outlay from the NPV. If the result is zero, we have made the correct guess—the IRR is equal to the rate guessed. If the result is not zero, we must guess a new rate and recompute the calculation. We repeat this procedure until we obtain a difference of zero.

A simple guessing method is to start arbitrarily high. As long as the NPV is higher than the initial outlay, we halve the next guess. Once the NPV becomes less than the initial outlay, we have bracketed the IRR between the two values. We should then continue guessing until the NPV and initial outlay become equal.

APPLICATION EXAMPLE

Let's assume that you are considering an investment that requires an initial cash outlay of $90,000, and brings cash flows of $15,000, $17,000, $19,000, and $125,000. Using these figures you want to compute the IRR.

SPREADSHEET INSTRUCTIONS

For this example we will set up a very simple VisiCalc form, as shown in Figure 3.15.

We guess the initial interest rate and enter it at B2. The NPV is then equal to:

```
A3:NPV
   B3: −A1 + @NPV(B2,B1.E1)
```

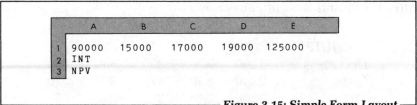

	A	B	C	D	E
1	90000	15000	17000	19000	125000
2	INT				
3	NPV				

Figure 3.15: Simple Form Layout

We continue guessing until the NPV approximates the initial cash outlay. We summarize this process in the following table:

INT	NPV
.300	-15988
.150	19859
.225	-581
.220	605
.223	-109

We can use an IRR of 22% since the NPV is close to zero.

The next example applies this method of computing the IRR to a more complex problem.

PROJECT SELECTION

Business firms often receive a greater number of requests for capital projects than they have available funds. One method that can be used to select the best projects from a list of requests is to calculate the IRR for each project, and then rank the projects according to their results. Businesses can then select those projects with suitable IRRs for funding, as long as sufficient capital is available.

APPLICATION EXAMPLE

Let's assume that your company is considering replacing several pieces of equipment. The initial cash outlays and projected after-tax cash flows appear below:

		YEAR			
EQUIP	COST	1	2	3	4
Drill Press	1200	300	320	340	360
Lathe	2700	850	875	890	910
Mill	2500	840	880	910	930
Router	1800	600	650	690	725

SPREADSHEET INSTRUCTIONS

Figures 3.16 and 3.17 show sample printouts for this example. Note that we purposely displayed the output twice. Figure 3.16 shows the results of guessing all of the IRRs at 25%; Figure 3.17 shows the results after the final iteration. For this example, we have prepared a very simple VisiCalc spreadsheet. The spreadsheet instructions appear in Figure 3.18. Let's now examine these instructions.

In this example, we determine the present value from the cash flows by using a formula of the type:

$$NPV = @NPV(I, YR1.YR4)$$

	A	B	C	D	E	F	G	H
1				PROJECT	SELECTION			
2							CASH FLOWS	
3	EQUIP	COST	NPV	IRR	1	2	3	4
4	DR PRESS	1200	1200	.038	300	320	340	360
5	LATHE	2700	2703	.114	850	875	890	910
6	MILL	3500	2500	.155	840	880	910	930
7	ROUTER	1800	1798	.172	600	650	690	725

Figure 3.16: PROJECT SELECTION—TRIAL IRR

	A	B	C	D	E	F	G	H
1				PROJECT	SELECTION			
2							CASH FLOWS	
3	EQUIP	COST	NPV	IRR	1	2	3	4
4	DR PRESS	1200	766	.25	300	320	340	360
5	LATHE	2700	2068	.25	850	875	890	910
6	MILL	3500	2082	.25	840	880	910	930
7	ROUTER	1800	1546	.25	600	650	690	725

Figure 3.17: PROJECT SELECTION—FINAL IRR

```
/CY
/GFI
D1:PROJECT          E1:SELECTION
A3:/FR
/R:B3.H3
A3:EQUIP
   A4:DR PRESS      A5:LATHE
   A6:MILL          A7:ROUTER
B3:COST
C3:NPV
   C4:@NPV(D4,E4.H4)
   /R:C5.C7:RRR
D3:IRR
D4:/FG
/R:D5.D7
G2:CASH FLOW        H2:S
   E3:1             F3:2                    G3:3                    H3:4
```

Figure 3.18: Spreadsheet Instructions: PROJECT SELECTION

where I is the IRR, which is guessed by using the procedure we discussed in the previous example. In this example we accept the IRR, which equates the present value and the project cost.

DISCOUNTED BONDS

When bonds are issued they can usually be purchased at very near par value. As market interest rates rise and fall so do the prices of bonds. Bonds are said to be purchasable at a discount rate when their price falls below par value. Since the rate of interest paid is fixed, the investor's yield rises. As the bond matures its price returns to par value, thus resulting in a capital gain. In this example, we will show one way of reviewing alternate choices of discounted bonds.

APPLICATION EXAMPLE

Let's assume that you are in the fifty percent tax bracket and are considering purchasing United States Treasury bonds. You wish to determine which of two bonds would be the better investment. The bond rates and prices are:

DATE	INTEREST	PRICE
MAY 85	10.37	86.80
MAY 85	14.37	96.14

Interest is paid twice a year at half the indicated rate. Tax is 50% on the interest received. During the final period you will also receive a capital gain. Tax is paid at the 50% rate, but only on 40% of the gain.

SPREADSHEET INSTRUCTIONS

Figure 3.19 shows the printout for this example. The spreadsheet instructions appear in Figure 3.20.

	A	B	C	D	E	F
1						
2			BOND	ANALYSIS		
3		INCOME	TAX	NET		
4	(10.37)	-86.80			IRR	.045
5	MAY 82	5.18	2.59	2.59	PV	86.80
6	NOV 82	5.18	2.59	2.59		
7	MAY 83	5.18	2.59	2.59		
8	NOV 83	5.18	2.59	2.59		
9	MAY 84	5.18	2.59	2.59		
10	NOV 84	5.18	2.59	2.59		
11	MAY 85	5.18	2.59	99.95		
12	MAY 85	100.00	2.64			
13						
14						
15						
16	(14.37)	-96.14				
17	MAY 82	7.15	3.58	3.58	IRR	.0416
18	NOV 82	7.15	3.58	3.58	PV	95.93
19	MAY 83	7.15	3.58	3.58		
20	NOV 83	7.15	3.58	3.58		
21	MAY 84	7.15	3.58	3.58		
22	NOV 84	7.15	3.58	3.58		
23	MAY 85	7.15	3.58	102.80		
24	MAY 85	100.00	0.77			

Figure 3.19: BOND ANALYSIS

```
/CY
/GF$
D2:BOND              E2:ANALYSIS
B3:/FR
/R:C3.D3
A4:''(10.37)
   A5:MAY 82        A6:NOV 82        A7:MAY 83        A8:NOV 83
   A9:MAY 84        A10:NOV 84       A11:MAY 85       A12:MAY 85
A16:''(14.37)
   A5:/R.A12:A17
B3:INCOME
   B4: —86.8
   B5:5.18
   /R:B6.B11
   B12:100
   B16: —96.14
   B17:7.15
   /R:B18.B23
   B24:100
C3:TAX
   C5: .5*B5
   /R:C6.C11:R
   /R:C17.C23:R
   C12: .4*.5*(B12+B4)
   C24: .4*.5*(B24+B16)
D3:NET
   D5: +B5—C5
   /R:D6.D10:RR
   /R:D17.D22:RR
   D11: +B11+B12—C11—C12
   D23: +B23+B24—C23—C24
E4:/FR IRR           E5:/FR   PV
   F5:/FG @NPV(F4,D5.D11)
E17:/FR IRR          E18:/FR   PV
   F18:@NPV(F17,D17.D23)
```

Figure 3.20: Spreadsheet Instructions: DISCOUNTED BONDS

In this example, we enter the interest received in column B. We compute the tax and net income on the first bond as follows:

```
C3:TAX
    C5: .5*B5
    /R:C6.C11:R
    C12: .4*.5*(B12+B4)
D3:NET
    D5: +B5-C5
    /R:D6.D10:RR
```

We enter the initial payment for the bond as a negative number, thus accounting for the plus (+) sign in the previous expression. We similarly enter the tax and income for the other bond.

Next, we set up a net present value calculation and use the iterative procedure to determine the IRR. This calculation shows the IRR for the deep-discounted bond at 4.5%, and the IRR for the higher priced bond at 4.1%. Thus, the deep-discounted bond is slightly more favorable. Note that since payments are received twice yearly, the actual IRR is about 9%.

ADDITIONAL REMARKS

This type of analysis is useful for many different investment situations. The key factor in making investment decisions among like investments is the tax consequence, which you can easily evaluate using the VisiCalc program. You may want to use this type of analysis to set up similar forms for common stock evaluations as well. For example, you can change the spreadsheet to compare stocks paying different dividend rates, and then assume various growth rates in the value of the stock. However, keep in mind that, unlike the case with bonds, this growth is not assured.

PORTFOLIO ANALYSIS

The VisiCalc program can be used as a simulation tool for analyzing alternative investments. With a properly set up investment table, it is possible to analyze various investment alternatives quickly. In this example, we will review an investment portfolio.

APPLICATION EXAMPLE

An investor desires to review an investment portfolio mix. His initial plan is to spread his capital in the following way:

- $200,000 in stocks that are currently paying a 10% dividend; dividends are expected to grow at a rate of 10% per year.
- $100,000 in trust deeds at 18% interest.
- $100,000 in CD's at 15% interest.
- $10,000 in money market funds at 14% interest.

The investor projects that interest rates will fall at a rate of 10% per year.

The investor also has an additional investment in tax-free bonds that is providing an 8% return. The investor's living expenses are $30,000 per year; he expects them to increase at a rate of 10% per year.

SPREADSHEET INSTRUCTIONS

Figure 3.21 shows a printout of the investment analysis form for this example. The spreadsheet instructions appear in Figure 3.22. Let's examine them.

	A	B	C	D	E	F	G
			INVESTMENT ANALYSIS				
1							
2							
3	INVSTMT	VALUE	YR1	YR2	YR3	YR4	YR5
4	TAXABLE						
5							
6	STOCKS	200000	20000	22000	24200	26620	29282
7	DEEDS	100000	18000	16200	14580	13122	11810
8	CDS	100000	15000	13500	12150	10935	9842
9	SAVINGS	10000	1400	1260	1134	1021	919
10	TOTAL	410000	54400	52960	52064	51698	51852
11							
12	TAX		27200	26480	26032	25849	25926
13							
14	BONDS	400000	32000	32000	32000	32000	32000
15							
16	INCOME		59200	58480	58032	57849	57926
17							
18	EXPENSES	30000	30000	33000	36300	39930	43923
19							
20	SAVINGS						
21	BALANCE	10000	39200	64680	86412	104331	118334

Figure 3.21: INVESTMENT ANALYSIS

```
/CY
/GFI
D1:INVESTMEN        E1:T ANALYSI        F1:S
A3:/FR
/R:B3.G3
A3:INVSTMT          B3:VALUE            C3:YR1              D3:YR2
E3:YR3              F3:YR4              G3:YR5
A4:TAXABLE
  A6:STOCKS
     C6: .1*B6
     D6:1.1*C6
     /R:E6.G6:R
  A7:DEEDS
     C7: .18*B7
     D7: .9*C7
     /R:E7.G7:R
  A8:CDS
     C8: .15*B8
     D8: .9*C8
     /R:E8.G8:R
  A9:SAVINGS
     C9: .14*B20
     D9: .9*C9
     /R:E9.G9:R
  A10:TOTAL
     B10:@SUM(B6.B9)
     /R:C10.G10:RR
  A12:TAX
     C12: .5*C10
     /R:D12.G12:R
  A14:BONDS
     C14: .08*B14
     /R:D14.G14:N
  A16:INCOME
```

Figure 3.22: Spreadsheet Instructions: INVESTMENT ANALYSIS (continues)

```
     C16:+C10−C12+C14
     /R:D16.G16:RRR
A18:EXPENSES
     C18:+B18
     D18:1.1*C18
     /R:E18.G18:R
A20:SAVINGS        A21:BALANCE
     C20:+B20+C16−C18
     /R:D20.G20:RRR
```

Figure 3.22: Spreadsheet Instructions: INVESTMENT ANALYSIS (cont.)

Taxable income consists of stock dividends and interest income. The common stocks dividend is 10% of the current value and grows at a rate of 10%. In this example, we express this as:

```
A6:STOCKS
     C6: .1*B6
     D6:1.1*C6
     /R:E6.G6:R
```

The deeds, CD's, and money market funds all pay interest on the current investment, but this interest is expected to fall. We write the CD income as:

```
A8:CDS
     C8: .15*B8
     D8: .9*C8
     /R:E8.G8:R
```

We write the other interest income in a similar way.

Next, we total the interest income and apply the tax:

```
A10:TOTAL
     B10:@SUM(B6.B9)
     /R:C10.G10:RR
A12:TAX
     C12: .5*C10
     /R:D12.G12:R
```

The interest from the bonds is nontaxable.

Next, we compute the bond income and add it to the net income we obtained above:

```
A14:BONDS
   C14: .08*B14
   /R:D14.G14:N
A16:INCOME
   C16:+C10−C12+C14
   /R:D16.G16:RRR
```

We write the investor's expenses as:

```
A18:EXPENSES
   C18:+B18
   D18:1.1*C18
   /R:E18.G18:R
```

Finally, we compute the rise or fall in the investor's savings balance by subtracting the expense totals from his income and adding the result to the savings balance:

```
A20:SAVINGS        A21:BALANCE
   C20:+B20+C16−C18
   /R:D20.G20:RRR
```

ADDITIONAL REMARKS

You can extend this technique to include any number of investments. Since uniform increases and decreases in the interest and dividend rates have been assumed, you can change the form to reflect a number of projected patterns. As an example, you could set up an identical grid to reflect actual income. The comparison of actual versus projected income can be a useful tool in deciding whether the portfolio mix should remain as is, or be modified in concert with changing economic conditions. You could also modify the form so that the savings balance is not allowed to rise above $10,000. You can do this by transferring excess funds to the savings account and allowing extra interest to be earned.

SUMMARY

In this chapter, we have learned to use the VisiCalc program in a number of financial situations. We have seen that it can be a very useful tool for performing tedious calculations, such as those done on financial statements and balance sheets. Many of the examples in this chapter have included NET PRESENT VALUE analyses. We have used the built-in @NPV function to develop powerful models in a variety of applications. For example, we have used this function to analyze cash flow streams and to calculate the IRR for a cash flow stream.

A BUDGETING SYSTEM

4

A BUDGETING SYSTEM

Budget Tables Sales Budget Production Budget
Projected Budgeted Income Statement
Cash Budget

OVERVIEW

In this chapter we will use the VisiCalc program to set up a company budgeting system. We will first create a sales forecast—then, we will prepare budgets for the sales and manufacturing departments. Finally, we will produce a cash plan and a budgeted income statement.

The examples in this chapter take advantage of the recomputation capability of the

VisiCalc program. You can change figures in the budget tables, and the VisiCalc program will automatically calculate new budget totals. VisiCalc makes it easy to explore the effects of various assumptions on a company's profitability.

BUDGET TABLES

Evaluating various budgeting alternatives can be a simple task when using the VisiCalc program. By placing in a parameter table all the variables that are subject to change, we can easily compute and recompute budgets by simply changing entries in the table.

APPLICATION EXAMPLE

Let's assume that you need to prepare a master budget for your company for the year 1982. You plan to use a parameter table to explore various alternatives in the following areas:

- sales
- manufacturing
- material purchases
- product pricing and cost
- other expense percentages
- accounts receivable timing

SPREADSHEET INSTRUCTIONS

Figure 4.1 shows a sample printout of a master budget. The spreadsheet instructions appear in Figure 4.2.

```
        A        B         C         D         E        F        G
 1                            MYCO INC.
 2                    415 WEST HARRISON STREET
 3                    JACKSON  CALIF.   94223
 4
 5                    MASTER   BUDGET                     DEC. 1981
 6  ================================================================
 7                    TABLES
 8
 9  SALES
10  ------------------        %        RATE
11  SALARY                    5        0.05
12  COMM                     10        0.10
13  ADVTG                     5        0.05
14  OTHER                     5        0.05
15
16  MANUF
17  ------------------        %        RATE
18  LABOR      RATE                       7
19  LABOR      OHD          100        1.00
20  MATL       OHD           10        0.10
21
22  MATERIAL  PURCHASE
23  ------------------        %        RATE
24  CURRENT   QUARTER        60        0.60
25  NEXT      QUARTER        40        0.40
26
27  PRODUCT   TABLE
28  ------------------
29                        PRICE    HOURS MATERIAL  GR RATE
30  CPU                    1400       10      300       10
31  DRIVE                   405        4      110        8
32  PRINTER                 695        9      135       15
33
34  OTHER     EXPENSE         %        RATE
35  ------------------
36  G&A                      10        0.10
37  TAX                      50        0.50
38
39  ACCOUNTS RCVBL
40  ------------------        %        RATE
41  CURRENT   QUARTER        70        0.70
42  PREVIOUS  QUARTER        30        0.30
```

Figure 4.1: A MASTER BUDGET

```
/CY
/SL MASTER.VC
/GFI
C5:MASTER          D5:BUDGET          G5:DEC.1981
B7:/FR TAB         C7:LES
```

Figure 4.2: Spreadsheet Instructions: A MASTER BUDGET (continues)

```
A9:SALES
A10:/— —              B10:/— —
A11:SALARY           A12:COMM          A13:ADVTG         A14:OTHER
    C10:/FR ''%
    D10:/FR RATE
        D11:/F$ +C11/100
        /R:D12.D14:R
A16:MANUF
A17:/— —              B17:/— —
A18:LABOR            B18:RATE
A19:LABOR            B19:OHD
A20:MATL             B20:OHD
    C17:/FR ''%
    D17:/FR RATE
        D19:/F$ +C19/100
        /R:D20:R
A22:MATERIAL         B22:PURCHASE
A23:/— —              B23:/— —
A24:CURRENT          B24:QUARTER
A25:NEXT             B25:QUARTER
    C23:/FR ''%
    D23:/FR RATE
        D24:/F$ +C24/100
        /R:D25:R
A27:PRODUCT          B27:TABLE
A28:/— —              B28:/— —
B29:/FR
/R:C29.E29
B29:PRICE            C29:HOURS         D29:MATERIAL      E29:GR RATE
A30:CPU
A31:DRIVE
A32:PRINTER
A34:OTHER            B34:EXPENSE       C34:/FR ''%       D34:/FR RATE
A35:/— —              B35:/— —
A36:G&A
```

Figure 4.2: Spreadsheet Instructions: A MASTER BUDGET (continues)

```
A37:TAX
     D36:/F$ +C36/100
     /R:D37:R
A39:ACCOUNTS      B39:RCVBL
A40:/ — —          B40:/ — —
A41:CURRENT       B41:QUARTER
A42:PREVIOUS      B42:QUARTER
     C40:/FR ''%
     D40:/FR RATE
       D41:/F$ +C41/100
       /R:D42:R
```

Figure 4.2: Spreadsheet Instructions: A MASTER BUDGET (cont.)

Let's now review the budget tables. We can see that in the sales table we express sales budget categories as a percentage of dollar sales. To speed computation we convert these figures to their decimal equivalents. The parameters in the table are salary, commission, advertising, and miscellaneous expenses.

In the manufacturing table we include entries for the labor rate, labor overhead rate, and the material overhead rate. We express the labor overhead rate as a percentage of labor dollars and the material overhead rate as a percentage of material purchase dollars. We use a labor rate that is an average of all manufacturing salaries on a dollars per hour basis.

In the table showing material purchases we calculate the percentage of materials to be bought in the current quarter in terms of the current and next quarter requirements. This allows the planner to correctly factor-in the lead time and the inventory cost effects.

The product table contains information on the products being manufactured. We include in this table the following items: the sales price, the manufacturing hours, the material cost per unit, and the sales growth rate. Also, in this display we include an additional table. This table accounts for any additional variable information, including the income tax rate and the general and administrative expense percentages.

Finally, in the accounts receivable table we include information about the collection period for accounts. Specifically, the table provides the percentage of billings collected in the current quarter, and the percentage collected in the previous quarter.

SALES BUDGET

Using data stored in the parameter table, we will now prepare a sales forecast and a sales expense budget.

APPLICATION EXAMPLE

Your company is in the computer manufacturing business. During the fourth quarter of the previous year, your company achieved the following sales figures:

PRODUCT	NO.	INCOME	PRICE/UNIT
CPUS	960	1,344,000	1400
DRIVES	470	190,000	405
PRINTERS	570	396,000	695

The total sales budget is to be 25% of the total sales. During the previous quarter, sales expenses ran:

SALARIES	127,632
COMMISSION	198,000
ADVERTISING	102,300
OTHER	107,195

We will now use these figures to prepare a sales budget for 1982.

SPREADSHEET INSTRUCTIONS

Figure 4.3 displays a printout of a budget for the sales division. The spreadsheet instructions appear in Figure 4.4. Note that we have saved all the budget spreadsheets on one VisiCalc disk file so that data can flow between the budget spreadsheets. Let's now examine the spreadsheet for the sales budget.

Figure 4.3: SALES DIVISION BUDGET

	Q4 (ACT)	Q1	Q2	Q3	Q4	Q1	Q2
UNITS							
CPUS	960	984	1009	1034	1060	1086	1113
DRIVES	470	479	489	499	509	519	529
PRINTERS	570	591	614	637	660	685	711
SALES (000'S)							
CPUS	1344	1378	1412	1447	1484	1521	1559
DRIVES	190	194	198	202	206	210	214
PRINTERS	396	411	426	442	459	476	494
TOTAL	1931	1983	2036	2092	2149	2207	2267
SALARIES	97	99	102	105	107	110	113
COMM	193	198	204	209	215	221	227
ADVTG	97	99	102	105	107	110	113
OTHER	97	99	102	105	107	110	113
TOTAL	483	496	509	523	537	552	567

```
J5:SALES              K5:BUDGET
I6:/—=
/R:J6.O6
I7:/FR                /R:J7.O7
I7:Q4      J7:Q1      K7:Q2    L7:Q3    M7:Q4    N7:Q1    O7:Q2
I8:/FR"(ACT)
H8:UNITS
H9:/——
  H10:CPUS
    J10:(1+(E30/4/100))*I10
    /R:K10.O10:NR
  H11:DRIVES
    J11:(1+(E31/4/100))*I11
    /R:K11.O11:NR
  H12:PRINTERS
    J12:(1+(E32/4/100))*I12
```

Figure 4.4: Spreadsheet Instructions: SALES BUDGET (continues)

```
        /R:K12.O12:NR
H14:SALES (00          I14:"0'S)
H15:/——
  H16:CPUS
    I16:+I10*B30/1000
      /R:J16.O16:RN
  H17:DRIVES
    I17:+I11*B31/1000
      /R:J17.O17:RN
  H18:PRINTERS
    I18:+I12*B32/1000
      /R:J18.O18:RN
  H19:TOTAL
    I19:@SUM(I16.I18)
      /R:J19.O19:RR
  H21:SALARIES
    I21:+D11*I19
      /R:J21.O21:NR
  H22:COMM
    I22:+D12*I19
      /R:J22.O22:NR
  H23:ADVTG
    I23:+D13*I19
      /R:J23.O23:NR
  H24:OTHER
    I24:+D14*I19
      /R:J24.O24:NR
  H25:TOTAL
    I25:@SUM(I21.I24)
      /R:J25.O25:RR
```

Figure 4.4: Spreadsheet Instructions: SALES BUDGET (cont.)

We begin preparation of the spreadsheet by entering the actual fourth quarter sales. The budget tables specify an annual growth rate, which we will use to determine the future sales of each unit. The CPU growth rate is stored at location E29. We divide this rate by four in order to convert it to a quarterly forecast. Thus, we express the projected growth rate as:

```
H10:CPUS
    J10:(1+(E30/4/100))*I10
    /R:K10.O10:NR
```

After projecting unit sales for the other products, we use the tables to convert these sales to sales dollars. For the CPUs, we write:

```
H16:CPUS
    I16:+I10*B30/1000
    /R:J16.O16:RN
```

In this calculation we convert the numbers to thousands to keep them readable. We then calculate the total dollar sales by adding the amounts for each product:

```
H19:TOTAL
    I19:@SUM(I16.I18)
    /R:J19.O19:RR
```

Next, we use the dollar sales forecast to budget the individual sales expense items. We pull the budget percentages from the tables to compute each line item. For example, we express the sales staffs' salaries as:

```
H21:SALARIES
    I21:+D11*I19
    /R:J21.O21:NR
```

The spreadsheet instructions are completed by writing the expressions for the other line items. The total sales budget is determined by obtaining the column sums.

When we have entered the instructions we can analyze the effects of alternate sales forecasts and of different budget percentages by varying the appropriate parameters.

ADDITIONAL REMARKS

The spreadsheet design in this example allows you to obtain variable sales budget percentages. For example, suppose that you need to lower the commission rate to 9%. By simply changing the commission percentage at D12, the VisiCalc program will automatically recompute the budget. Remember, it is important to store those parameters that are frequently varied in a parameter table.

PRODUCTION BUDGET

Once we have completed a sales forecast, we can develop a production budget. A budgeting system works best if *all* the budgets are entered on the same spreadsheet. By doing this, we can easily make changes that involve the recomputation of the entire budget.

In actual practice, department managers will probably complete their budgets on individual diskettes—and as long as their columns do not overlap, these files can then be loaded, one at a time, into the computer system and combined on a single spreadsheet.

APPLICATION EXAMPLE

Using the input from the sales forecast, you wish to forecast labor, overhead, and material costs for the production department. For this example you make the following assumptions:

1. Beginning inventory per quarter is to be one-half of the sales forecast for that quarter.

2. Materials are to be ordered so that 40% of the necessary materials are received in the previous quarter and 60% in the current quarter.

3. Factory labor rate and the unit materials cost are entered in the production table.

4. Manufacturing overhead is computed at 100% on labor and 10% on materials.

You enter these requirements into the tables specified in the previous examples.

SPREADSHEET INSTRUCTIONS

Figure 4.5 shows a sample printout of a production budget. Note that the production budget is divided into several component parts. Figure 4.6 shows the spreadsheet instructions for this budget. Let's examine these instructions.

	Q	R	S	T	U	V	W	X
5			PRODUCTION BUDGET (000'S)					
6	===
7			UNIT INVENTORY					
8		Q4	Q1	Q2	Q3	Q4	Q5	Q6
9	BEGIN							
10	CPU		492	504	517	530	543	557
11	DRIVE		240	244	249	254	259	265
12	PRINTER		296	307	318	330	343	355
13								
14	END							
15	CPU	492	504	517	530	543	557	
16	DRIVE	240	244	249	254	259	265	
17	PRINTER	296	307	318	330	343	355	
18								
19			UNIT PRODUCTION					
20	CPU		996	1021	1047	1073	1100	
21	DRIVE		484	494	504	514	524	
22	PRINTER		602	625	648	673	698	
23								
24								
25			MANUFACTURING COST					
26								
27	LABOR		121	125	128	132	136	
28								
29	MATLS		433	445	457	469	482	
30	OHD		165	169	174	179	184	
31	TOTAL		719	739	759	780	801	

	AA	AB	AC	AD
6	=======================================
7		MATERIALS PURCHASE	BUDGET	
8	Q1	Q2	Q3	Q4
9	438	450	462	474
10				
11		INVENTORY VALUE		
12	1018	1046	1074	1103

Figure 4.5: PRODUCTION BUDGET

```
/CY
/SL BUDGET.VC
O6:/R:P6.AD6
S5:PRODUCTIO        T5:N BUDGET          U5:''(000'S)
S7:UNIT INVE        T7:NTORY
Q8:/FR
/R:R8.Y8
R8:Q4    S8:Q1    T8:Q2    U8:Q3    V8:Q4    W8:Q5    X8:Q6
   Q9:BEGIN
      Q10:CPU
         S10: .5*J10
         /R:T10.X10:R
      Q11:DRIVE
         S11: .5*J11
         /R:T11.X11:R
      Q12:PRINTER
         S12: .5*J12
         /R:T12.X12:R
   Q14:END
      Q15:CPU
         R15: .5*J10
         /R:S15.W15:R
      Q16:DRIVE
         R16: .5*J11
         /R:S16.W16:R
      Q17:PRINTER
         R17: .5*J12
         /R:S17.W17:R
   S19:UNIT PROD        T19:UCTION
      Q20:CPU
         S20:+J10+S15−S10
         /R:T20.W20:RRR
      Q21:DRIVE
         S21:+J11+S16−S11
         /R:T21.W21:RRR
      Q22:PRINTER
         S22:+J12+S17−S12
```

Figure 4.6: Spreadsheet Instructions: PRODUCTION BUDGET (continues)

```
        /R:T22.W22:RRR
S25:MANUFACTU      T25:RING COST
    Q27:LABOR
        S27: +D18/1000*((S20*C30)+(S21*C31)+(S22*C32))
        /R:T27.W27:N RN RN RN
    Q29:MATLS
        S29:((S20*D30)+(S21*D31)+(S22*D32))/1000
        /R:T29.W29:RNRNRN
    Q30:OHD
        S30:(S27*D19)+(S29*D20)
        /R:T30.W30:RNRN
    Q31:TOTAL
        S31:@SUM(S27.S30)
        /R:T31.W31:RR
AB7:MATERIALS      AC7:" PURCHASE     AD7:" BUDGET
AA8:/FR
/R:AB8.AD8
AA8:Q1          AB8:Q2          AC8:Q3          AD8:Q4
    AA9:(D24*S29)+(D25*T29)
    /R:AB9.AD9:NRNR
AB11:INVENTORY     AC11:" VALUE
    AA12:((B30*S15)+(B31*S16)+(B32*S17))/1000
    /R:AB12.AD12:NRNRNR
```

Figure 4.6: Spreadsheet Instructions: PRODUCTION BUDGET (cont.)

In this example, we are required to establish a beginning inventory that is one-half the production forecast. For CPUs, the first quarter forecast appears in coordinate J10. The correct formula for the beginning inventory is:

```
    Q9:BEGIN
    Q10:CPU
        S10: .5*J10
        /R:T10.X10:R
```

We express the first quarter drive and printer inventory by using similar calculations. We replicate this procedure for the next four quarters.

The ending inventory is simply the beginning inventory for the next quarter. Thus, we write:

```
Q14:END
   Q15:CPU
      R15: .5*J10
      /R:S15.W15:R
```

We can calculate the production requirements in any quarter by calculating the units shipped, plus the change in inventory. We specify the first quarter production as:

```
Q20:CPU
   S20: +J10+S15−S10
   /R:T20.W20:RRR
```

We replicate this formula for all of the quarters. We similarly calculate other production requirements.

Next, we calculate the manufacturing cost by using the unit production figures and the manufacturing cost tables. Labor cost is budgeted as:

(Standard Rate)*(Units Produced)*(Hours per Unit)

We calculate CPU labor as:

D18*S20*C30/1000

Thus, the expression

```
Q27:LABOR
   S27: +D18/1000*((S20*C30)+(S21*C31)+(S22*C32))
```

yields the total labor for all the units produced. We divide the labor figure by 1000 so that the production budget will be printed in 000's.

Likewise, we write the materials cost as:

```
Q29:MATLS
   S29:((S20*D30)+(S21*D31)+(S22*D32))/1000
```

Manufacturing overhead is 100% on labor and 10% on materials. Again using the table, we express the overhead as:

```
Q30:OHD
   S30:(S27*D19)+(S29*D20)
   /R:T30.W30:RNRN
```

We complete the first quarter production budget by adding the figures for the labor, materials, and overhead:

```
Q31:TOTAL
   S31:@SUM(S27.S30)
   /R:T31.W31:RR
```

We replicate these formulas for the other quarters.

Lastly, we compute for the first quarter the materials purchase budget and the inventory value at retail. When we calculate the materials purchase budget we make use of the tables already established. Unfortunately, we must use figures from the next quarter. In order to avoid a forward reference, we must make sure that the data for the next quarter has already been calculated by the VisiCalc program. We do this by putting the materials budget in column AA, to the right of the production budget. Thus, to calculate:

$$\text{Materials} = .4*(\text{Next Quarter}) + .6*(\text{This Quarter})$$

we write:

```
AA9:(D24*S29)+(D25*T29)
   /R:AB9.AD9:NRNR
```

where D24 and D25 contain the material purchase percentages, and S28 and T28 contain the percentages for the current and next quarter material requirements.

We express the inventory value as the sum of the ending inventories multiplied by their prices:

```
AA12:((B30*S15)+(B31*S16)+(B32*S17))/1000
   /R:AB12.AD12:NRNRNR
```

ADDITIONAL REMARKS

You have now completed a production budget. Because it is included on the same spreadsheet with the sales budget, any change you now make to the sales forecasts will result in an immediate recalculation of the production budget. Because the manufacturing labor rates and material costs are included in a table, any change in costs will result in an immediate recomputation of the budget.

BUDGETED INCOME STATEMENT

APPLICATION EXAMPLE

You now want to prepare a budgeted income statement for an entire year. You plan to do this by combining various elements of the sales and manufacturing budgets, and adding general and administrative expenses.

SPREADSHEET INSTRUCTIONS

A completed printout of a budgeted income statement appears in Figure 4.7. Let's examine the spreadsheet instructions that produced it. They appear in Figure 4.8. Note that the first quarter projections are made and calculated across the sheet.

	AI	AJ	AK	AL	AM	AN	AO
1							
2							
3							
4							
5			INCOME STATEMENT				
6	==
7			Q1	Q2	Q3	Q4	YR
8	SALES		1983	2036	2092	2149	8260
9	COST		719	739	759	780	2997
10	GROSS P		1263	1298	1333	1369	5262
11							
12							
13	SELLING		496	509	523	537	2065
14	G&A		198	204	209	215	826
15							
16	NET BT		569	585	600	617	2371
17							
18	TAX		285	292	300	308	1186
19							
20	NET		285	292	300	308	1186

Figure 4.7: INCOME STATEMENT

```
/CY
/SL BUDGET.VC
AD6:/R:AE6.AO6
AK5:INCOME ST        AL5:ATEMENT
AI7:/FR
/R:AK7.AP7
    AK7:Q1              AL7:Q2              AM7:Q3              AN7:Q4
AI8:SALES
    AK8:+J19
    /R:AL8.AN8:R
AI9:COST
    AK9:+S31
    /R:AL9.AN9:R
AI10:GROSS P
    AK10:+AK8—AK9
    /R:AL10.AN10:RR
AI13:SELLING
    AK13:+J25
    /R:AL13.AN13:R
AI14:G&A
    AK14:+D36*AK8
    /R:AL14.AN14:NR
AI16:NET BT
    AK16:+AK10—AK13—AK14
    /R:AL16.AN16:RRR
AI18:TAX
    AK18:+D37*AK16
    /R:AL18.AN18:NR
AI20:NET
    AK20:+AK16—AK18
    /R:AL20.AN20:RR
AO7:YR
    AO8:@SUM(AK8.AN8)
    /R:AO9.AO1O:RR
    /R:AO13.AO14:RR
    /R:AO16:RR
    /R:AO18:RR
    /R:AO20:RR
```

*Figure 4.8: Spreadsheei Instructions: **PROJECTED INCOME STATEMENT***

Sales are obtained directly from the sales forecast. Thus, we write:

```
AI8:SALES
   AK8:+J19
   /R:AL8.AN8:R
```

The cost of sales is the sum of the figures for manufacturing labor, overhead, and direct materials:

```
AI9:COST
   AK9:+S31
   /R:AL9.AN9:R
```

We can compute the gross profit by subtracting the cost of sales from the budgeted income:

```
AI10:GROSS P
   AK10:+AK8−AK9
   /R:AL10.AN10:RR
```

The selling expense has been budgeted and appears in location J25. Thus, we write:

```
AI13:SELLING
   AK13:+J25
   /R:AL13.AN13:R
```

We have not prepared a detailed general and administrative expense budget. We express this expense as a percentage in the budget tables. We write this as:

```
AI14:G&A
   AK14:+D36*AK8
   /R:AL14.AN14:NR
```

Next, we obtain the net income before tax by subtracting the selling expense and the G&A from the gross profit:

```
AI16:NET BT
   AK16:+AK10−AK13−AK14
   /R:AL16.AN16:RRR
```

Next, we calculate the income tax and subtract it from the before-tax income to arrive at the bottom line projection. We obtain the rate from the table.

AI18:TAX

AK18: +D37*AK16

/R:AL18.AN18:NR

AI20:NET

AK20: +AK16—AK18

/R:AL20.AN20:RR

ADDITIONAL REMARKS

For this example, we have made the assumption that all costs are expensed as they are incurred. Thus, on the income statement we have included manufacturing expenses for the month they occur. An alternate method used in many companies is to make manufactured items a part of a work-in-process inventory— whereby, they go to inventory and are shipped as they are needed. When this accounting method is used, the cost of sales is figured on a cost per unit basis, as each unit is shipped.

If you wish, you may extend the manufacturing table to include a standard cost per unit. For example, you can express the standard cost of a CPU as:

CPU Cost = (Labor Rate)*Hours + Materials

Or, you can also include this information—the CPU cost with labor and material overhead applied—in the table.

To figure the cost of sales for an income statement, you simply multiply the number of units shipped by the standard cost — rather than the actual hours and materials expended, as we have done in this example.

CASH BUDGET

We will now continue with the budgeting process.

APPLICATION EXAMPLE

You are now in a position to determine the cash required to operate your business. In the current example the sales budget is

25% of the total sales, the manufacturing budget is 40%, and the general and administrative expenses are 10%. The company has no short term debts; therefore, there are no interest payments.

For this example, you make two additional assumptions. You assume that:

1. the manufacturing overhead contains a depreciation expense of $10,000—a non-cash expense

2. collections on accounts receivable are:

   30 days — 20%
   60 days — 60%
   90 days — 20%

This latter assumption means that 70% of the receivables are collected in the current quarter and 30% in the following quarter.

SPREADSHEET INSTRUCTIONS

A printout of a sample cash plan appears in Figure 4.9. The spreadsheet instructions appear in Figure 4.10. To facilitate

	BA	BB	BC	BD	BE
1					
2					
3					
4					
5			CASH PLAN		
6	==				
7		Q1	Q2	Q3	Q4
8					
9	BEG CASH	**100**	374	656	945
10	RECEIPTS	1967	2020	2075	2132
11	TOTALS	2067	2395	2731	3076
12					
13	MATERIALS	438	450	462	474
14	DIR LABOR	121	125	128	132
15	MAN OHD	165	169	174	179
16	SALES EXP	496	509	523	537
17	G&A	198	204	209	215
18	TAX	285	292	300	308
19	TOTAL	1703	1749	1796	1845
20	DIFF	364	646	935	1231
21	DEPR	10	10	10	10
22					
23	END CASH	374	656	945	1241

Figure 4.9: CASH PLAN

information interchange, we continue the instructions on the
same spreadsheet as the other examples in this chapter. Let's now
examine these instructions.

```
/CY
/SL BUDGET.VC
AO6:/R:AP6.BE6
BD5:CASH PLAN
   BB7:/FR
   /R:BC7.BE7
   BB7:Q1              BC7:Q2              BD7:Q3              BE7:Q4
BA9:BEG CASH
   BC9:+BB23
   /R:BD9.BE9:R
BA10:RECEIPTS
   BB10:+D42*I19+(D41*J19)
   /R:BC10.BE10:NRNR
BA11:TOTALS
   BB11:+BB9+BB10
   /R:BC11.BE11:RR
BA13:MATERIALS
   BB13:+AA9
   /R:BC13.BE13:R
BA14:DIR LABOR
   BB14:+S27
   /R:BC14.BE14:R
BA15:MAN OHD
   BB15:+S30
   /R:BC15.BE15:R
BA16:SALES EXP
   BB16:+J25
   /R:BC16.BE16:R
BA17:G&A
   BB17:+AK14
   /R:BC17.BE17:R
```

Figure 4.10: Spreadsheet Instructions: CASH BUDGET (continues)

```
BA18:TAX
    BB18:+AK18
    /R:BC18.BE18:R
BA19:TOTAL
    BB19:@SUM(BB13.BB18)
    /R:BC19.BE19:RR
BA20:DIFF
    BB20:+BB11−BB19
    /R:BC20.BE20:RR
BA21:DEPR
    BB21:10
    /R:BC21.BE21
BA23:END CASH
    BB23:+BB20+BB21
    /R:BC23.BE23:RR
```

Figure 4.10: Spreadsheet Instructions: CASH BUDGET (cont.)

For this example, we assume the beginning cash balance to be $100,000. Receipts per quarter are 30% of the previous quarter's sales and 70% of the current quarter's sales. These percentages are listed in the budget tables at coordinates D39 and D40. For the first quarter we express cash receipts as:

```
BA10:RECEIPTS
    BB10:+D42*I19+(D41*J19)
    /R:BC10.BE10:NRNR
```

Material, labor, overhead, sales expense, G&A, and tax are all current expenses and are directly transferred from other parts of the sheet.

We can obtain the ending cash balance by adding the initial cash to the receipts, then subtracting the above disbursements, and finally, adding back depreciation, since it is a non-cash expense.

To compute available cash, we write:

```
BA11:TOTALS
    BB11:+BB9+BB10
    /R:BC11.BE11:RR
```

To calculate disbursements, we write:

```
BA19:TOTAL
  BB19:@SUM(BB13.BB18)
  /R:BC19.BE19:RR
```

To determine ending cash, we write:

```
BA23:END CASH
  BB23:+BB20+BB21
  /R:BC23.BE23:RR
```

The ending cash balance now becomes the beginning cash balance for the next quarter.

SUMMARY

In this chapter, we have developed and specified a complete budgeting system. We have designed the system so that all of the budgets are included on one spreadsheet—thus, any change in the sales budget will be immediately transferred to all the other budgets. In addition, we have used parameter tables in the manufacturing budget which allow for a quick evaluation of changes in labor rates or material costs.

5
SALES

Compound Growth   Seasonal Forecast   Sales Analysis
Salesperson Analysis   Quotation Preparation
Sales Forecast—Pricing Model   Sales Forecast—
Maturity Curve   Sales Forecast—Linear Regression

OVERVIEW

In many of the examples in previous chapters we have assumed that future sales projections have been available for use in calculations. In this chapter we will prepare such projections by using a variety of forecasting methods. In addition, we will develop VisiCalc spreadsheets for various record-keeping applications in the sales field.

In the first example we will prepare a forecast that is based on the assumption that sales will grow by a known percentage each year. This example demonstrates the effect of compound growth on a market, and on a particular company's share of the market.

In the second example we will develop a sales forecast for a business that participates in a seasonal market. For this example we will assume that a past record of data is available for review, and we will use it to develop a seasonal index from which we will prepare a forecast.

In the next example we will develop a spreadsheet that is useful for determining the profit contributions of individual items in a product line.

In the fourth example we will develop a spreadsheet that calculates the performance ratio of sales people throughout an organization. Although there are many different ways to evaluate this information, the example presented here provides useful guidelines for further analyses.

In the next example we will prepare a job cost proposal that provides cost quotations. Such quotations are useful for determining the potential costs of specific projects.

In the final examples we will review several mathematical methods that are useful for preparing sales forecasts. We will develop three spreadsheets: one showing supply and demand; one based on "S" curves for forecasting sales growth; and one using the mathematical technique, linear regression, for smoothing historical data.

COMPOUND GROWTH

A common forecasting method is to make projections based on compound growth (i.e., growth by a given percentage each year). In this example, we will make such forecasts.

APPLICATION EXAMPLE

Let's assume that your company is preparing its annual sales forecast. It participates in a market that is growing at a rate of 15% per year, and your company's current market share is 5%. In five years, this share is expected to reach 20%. You need to prepare a sales forecast that projects the total market volume and your company's share of the market for the next five years.

SPREADSHEET INSTRUCTIONS

A printout of a completed sales forecast appears in Figure 5.1. Recall that the design layout of a spreadsheet is an important factor when preparing useful forecasts and budgets with the VisiCalc program. For example, including a parameter table enhances the useability of a report, and makes it easier for the user to make variations in assumptions, and, thus, prepare new forecasts. In this example we place the figures for the initial market volume, the market growth rate, and the company's initial and final market share in a parameter table.

Figure 5.2 displays the spreadsheet instructions. Let's examine them.

```
         A        B        C        D        E        F        G
 1                             MYCO INC.
 2                    415 WEST HARRISON STREET
 3                    JACKSON  CALIF.   94223
 4
 5                    SALES    FORECAST                   JAN. 1982
 6       ===========================================================
 7
 8         TOTAL    MARKET     20.00
 9         GROWTH   RATE %     15.00
10
11         INITIAL  SHARE %     5.00
12         FINAL    SHARE %    20.00
13
14                           FORECAST  (000'S)
15                    1982     1983     1984     1985     1986
16         TOTAL     20.00    23.00    26.45    30.42    34.98
17
18         MYCO %     5.00     8.75    12.50    16.25    20.00
19         MYCO VOL   1.00     2.01     3.31     4.94     7.00
```

Figure 5.1: SALES FORECAST

```
/CY
/SL MASTER.VC
/GF$
C5:SALES          D5:FORECAST        G5:JAN. 1982
B8:TOTAL          C8:MARKET
B9:GROWTH         C9:RATE %
B11:INITIAL       C11:SHARE %
B12:FINAL         C12:SHARE %
D14:FORECAST      E14:"(000'S)
    C15:/FI
    /R:D15.G15
    C15:1982      D15:1983      E15:1984      F15:1985      G15:1986
    B16:TOTAL
       C16:+D8
       D16:+C16*(1+(D9/100))
       /R:E16.G16:RN
    B18:MYCO %
```

Figure 5.2: Spreadsheet Instructions: SALES FORECAST (continues)

```
        C18:+D11
        D18:(D12-D11)/4+C18
        /R:E18.G18:NNR
    B19:MYCO VOL
        C19:+C18/100*C16
        /R:D19.G19:RR
```
Figure 5.2: Spreadsheet Instructions: SALES FORECAST (cont.)

The instruction

      C16:+D8

copies the first year's market volume from the parameter table. Since we initially stored the growth rate in the table as a percent, we will convert it to decimal notation.

Next, we express the second year's volume as the first year's volume, plus the percentage growth:

      Volume(2) = Volume(1) + % * Volume(1)

In VisiCalc notation, we write:

      D16:+C16*(1+(D9/100))

Note that the sales growth changes as we change the percentage in the parameter table (by varying D9). We replicate the above formula for later years by writing:

      /R:E16.G16:RN

Next, we forecast the percentage growth for the company. We obtain the percentage for the first year by copying it from the parameter table. We then obtain percentages for subsequent years by calculating the growth per year and adding this result to the previous year's forecast. We compute the growth per year as:

      (Final Share − Initial Share)/4

In VisiCalc notation, we write:

      B18:MYCO %

        C18:+D11

        D18:(D12−D11)/4+C18

        /R:E18.G18:NNR

Next, we find the company's volume by multiplying the total year's volume by the company's share. We write this as:

      B19:MYCO VOL

        C19:+C18/100*C16

        /R:D19.G19:RR

ADDITIONAL REMARKS

You can prepare an alternate forecast by simply changing the percentages in the parameter table. Figure 5.3 shows a second report in which we have changed the overall market growth rate to 17%, and the company's final share to 25%.

```
       A        B        C        D        E        F        G
1                          MYCO INC.
2                  415 WEST HARRISON STREET
3                  JACKSON  CALIF.   94223
4
5                  SALES    FORECAST                  JAN. 1982
6  ================================================================
7
8        TOTAL    MARKET      20.00
9        GROWTH   RATE %      17.00
10
11       INITIAL  SHARE %      5.00
12       FINAL    SHARE %     25.00
13
14                         FORECAST  (000'S)
15                  1982     1983     1984     1985     1986
16       TOTAL     20.00    23.40    27.38    32.03    37.48
17
18       MYCO %     5.00    10.00    15.00    20.00    25.00
19       MYCO VOL   1.00     2.34     4.11     6.41     9.37
```

Figure 5.3: MODIFIED SALES FORECAST

PLOTTING THE DATA

You can often use a computer graphics program to plot VisiCalc spreadsheets. For this example we will use the VisiPlot™ program to graph the data appearing on the spreadsheet in Figure 5.2. To do this, we need to create three series in DIF format: market volume, MYCO volume, and MYCO market share. We specify market volume by writing:

C16:

/S#S

VOL. DIF

C20

C

We can create the other series in the same way and then use them as inputs to the VisiPlot program and create the graph. Figure 5.4 shows the graph for the sales forecast.

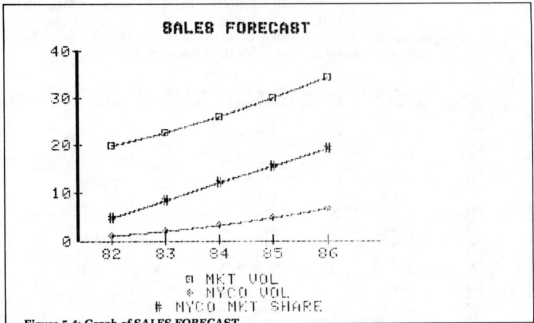

Figure 5.4: Graph of SALES FORECAST

SEASONAL FORECAST

Many businesses experience sales patterns that are highly seasonal in nature. For example, the retail industry experiences heavy sales during the Christmas season; farming and tourism also follow seasonal variations in sales. For this example we will use historical data to forecast future sales.

APPLICATION EXAMPLE

Your company has recorded and maintained a sales history on a quarterly basis for the past four years. You now wish to use this information to forecast future sales by preparing a report that summarizes past sales data and projects sales for the next four years. Because it is important to take seasonal variations into account when forecasting sales, you need to compute a seasonal index from the available historical sales data.

SPREADSHEET INSTRUCTIONS

We can determine a seasonal index from the ratio of sales for a given quarter when compared with the total sales for that year by computing the ratios by quarter for each year and then averaging their totals. We can then use these indices to prepare a seasonal sales forecast. An example of a seasonal forecast appears in Figure 5.5. The spreadsheet instructions for this example appear in Figure 5.6. Let's examine these instructions.

	A	B	C	D	E	F	G
1				MYCO INC.			
2			415 WEST HARRISON STREET				
3			JACKSON CALIF. 94223				
4							
5			SALES	FORECAST		JUN. 1981	
6	==						
7							
8			SALES	HISTORY			
9							
10		1978	1979	1980	1981		
11	WINTER	210.00	230.00	281.60	319.70		
12	SPRING	230.00	241.50	294.40	333.60		
13	SUMMER	160.00	195.50	217.60	222.40		
14	FALL	400.00	483.00	486.40	514.30		
15		-----------------------------------					
16	TOTAL	1000.00	1150.00	1280.00	1390.00		
17							
18			YEARLY	INDEX		AVERAGE	
19	WINTER	0.21	0.20	0.22	0.23	0.22	
20	SPRING	0.23	0.21	0.23	0.24	0.23	
21	SUMMER	0.16	0.17	0.17	0.16	0.17	
22	FALL	0.40	0.42	0.38	0.37	0.39	
23							
24	GRTH RATE		0.15	0.11	0.09	0.12	
25							
26			PROJECTION				
27		1982	1983	1984	1985		
28	TOTAL	1551.69	1732.20	1933.70	2158.64		
29	WINTER	333.61	372.42	415.75	464.11		
30	SPRING	353.01	394.08	439.92	491.09		
31	SUMMER	256.03	285.81	319.06	356.18		
32	FALL	609.04	679.89	758.98	847.27		

Figure 5.5: SEASONAL FORECAST

```
        /CY
        /GOR
        /GF$
        /SL MASTER.VC
        C5:SALES            D5:FORECAST         G5:JUN. 1981
        C8:SALES            D8:HISTORY
           B10:/FI
           /R:C10.E10
           B10:1978         C10:1979            D10:1980            E10:1981
           A11:WINTER       A12:SPRING          A13:SUMMER          A14:FALL
           B15:/— —
           /R:C15.E15
           A16:TOTAL
              B16:@SUM(B11.B14)
              /R:C16.E16:RR
        C18:YEARLY      D18:INDEX
           A19:WINTER
              B19:+B11/B16
              /R:C19.E19:RR
           A20:SPRING
              B20:+B12/B16
              /R:C20.E20:RR
           A21:SUMMER
              B21:+B13/B16
              /R:C21.E21:RR
           A22:FALL
              B22:+B14/B16
              /R:C22.E22:RR
           F18:/FR AVERAGE
              F19:@AVE(B19.E19)
              /R:F20.F22:RR
        A24:GRTH RATE
           C24:(C16—B16)/B16
           /R:D24.E24:RRR
           F24:@AVE(C24.E24)
```

Figure 5.6: Spreadsheet Instructions: SEASONAL FORCAST (continues)

```
C26:PROJECTIO        D26:N
   B27:/FI
   /R:C27.E27
   B27:1982          C27:1983          D27:1984          E27:1985
A28:TOTAL
      B28:+E16*(1+F24)
      C28:+B28*(1+F24)
      /R:D28.E28:RN
A29:WINTER
      B29:+F19*B28
      /R:C29.E29:NR
A30:SPRING
      B30:+F20*B28
      /R:C30.E30:NR
A31:SUMMER
      B31:+F21*B28
      /R:C31.E31:NR
A32:FALL
      B32:+F22*B28
      /R:C32.E32:NR
```

Figure 5.6: Spreadsheet Instructions: SEASONAL FORECAST (cont.)

We can use annual sales figures to determine the overall sales growth of an organization. There are several methods for forecasting future growth, based on this data. Here, we use the compound growth method developed in the previous example: We average the growth rate per year to obtain the overall average growth rate that we use in the forecast.

The first index we compute is for the winter of 1978:

Index = (Winter Sales)/Total Sales

Thus, in VisiCalc notation, we write:

B19:+B11/B16

We then replicate this computation to obtain the balance of the winter indexes:

/R:C19.E19:RR

We compute the other seasonal indexes in the same way.

We calculate the overall index for each season by averaging the individual yearly indexes. The @AVERAGE function provided by the VisiCalc program makes this a simple process. (See Appendix A for an explanation of this function.) Thus, we write:

```
F18/FR: AVERAGE
  F19:@AVE(B19.E19)
  /R:F20.F22:RR
```

(*Note:* if your computer does not accept the abbreviation, AVE, try the word AVERAGE.)

We can compute the growth rate for each year by using a simple percentage method:

$$\text{Growth Rate} = (\text{Sales2} - \text{Sales1})/\text{Sales1}$$

In VisiCalc notation, we write:

```
A24:GRTH RATE
  C24:(C16−B16)/B16
  /R:D24.E24:RRR
```

Next, we assume that the overall growth rate is the average of the yearly rates, and we indicate it as:

```
F24:@AVE(C24.E24)
```

Now that we have figures for the indexes and the average growth rate, we can complete our seasonal forecast.

We can project the growth in total sales by multiplying the growth rate by the annual sales:

```
A28:TOTAL
  B28:+E16*(1+F24)
  C28:+B28*(1+F24)
  /R:D28.E28:RN
```

ADDITIONAL REMARKS

In general, a simple method to use when preparing forecasts with cyclical data is to compute seasonal indexes. An alternate method for preparing this forecast is to compute the seasonal indexes, and then forecast the overall sales growth based on the linear regression method. We illustrate this method later on in this chapter.

SALES ANALYSIS

The VisiCalc program can be useful for conducting analyses of various sales patterns. We will now use it to generate a spreadsheet that allows for a detailed review of product sales and profit patterns.

APPLICATION EXAMPLE

A manufacturer wishes to analyze the sales patterns of his line of portable electric tools. The following table summarizes the average sales price and manufacturing cost of each item:

PRODUCT TABLE

ITEM	PRICE	COST
Drills	18.75	9.00
Circular saw	23.25	11.00
Jig saw	19.50	12.25
Router	31.75	15.00
Sander	25.50	10.25
Grinder	37.25	21.00

We will allocate the company's fixed expenses of $42,500 per month to each of the tools, based on the number of each type of tool sold.

SPREADSHEET INSTRUCTIONS

Figure 5.7 shows a printout of the output from the sales analysis display. The spreadsheet instructions for this display appear in Figure 5.8. Let's examine them.

```
            A         B         C         D         E         F         G         H
 1                                    MYCO INC.
 2                        415 WEST HARRISON STREET
 3                        JACKSON   CALIF.   94223
 4
 5                              SALES ANALYSIS                    FEB. 1982
 6  ==========================================================================
 7       ITEM      UNITS     SALES       %        GP            % NET PROF        %
 8
 9  DRILLS        1000      18750     17.36    9750.00      18.07    -192.52     -1.67
10  CIRC SAW       750      17438     16.15    9187.50      17.02    1731.36     15.10
11  JIG SAW        600      11700     10.83    4350.00       8.06   -1614.91    -14.08
12  ROUTER         400      12700     11.76    6700.00      12.41    2723.39     23.75
13  SANDER         800      20400     18.89   12200.00      22.61    4246.78     37.03
14  GRINDER        725      27006     25.01   11781.25      21.83    4573.65     39.88
15
16  TOTAL         4275     107994    100.00   53968.75     100.00   11469.75    100.00
17
18
19
20
21
22
23
24              PRODUCT   TABLE
25                PRICE      COST
26  DRILLS        18.75      9.00
27  CIRC SAW      23.25     11.00
28  JIG SAW       19.50     12.25
29  ROUTER        31.75     15.00
30  SANDER        25.50     10.25
31  GRINDER       37.25     21.00
32
33  FIXED EXP  42500.00
```

Figure 5.7: SALES ANALYSIS

```
/CY
/SL MASTER.VC
/GF$
C5:SALES          D5:ANALYSIS       G5:FEB. 1982
    A7:/FR
    /R:B7.H7
    A7:ITEM
    B7:UNITS
       B9:/FI
       /R:B10.B14
    A9:DRILLS         A10:CIRC SAW      A11:JIG SAW
```

Figure 5.8: Spreadsheet Instructions: SALES ANALYSIS (continues)

```
        A12:ROUTER          A13:SANDER          A14:GRINDER
      B24:PRODUCT          C24:TABLE
        A25:/FR
        /R:B25.C25
        A9:/R.A14:A26
        B25:PRICE          C25:COST
        A33:FIXED EXP
        C7:SALES
          C9:/FI +B9*B26
          /R:C10.C14:RR
        D7:'' %
          D9:100*C9/C16
          /R:D10.D14:RN
        E7:GP
          E9:+B9*(B26—C26)
          /R:E10.E14:RRR
        F7:'' %
          F9:100*E9/E16
          /R:F10.F14:RN
        G7:NET PROF
          G9:+E9—(B9/B16*B33)
          /R:G10.G14:RRNN
        H7:'' %
          H9:100*G9/G16
          /R:H10.H14:RN
        A16:TOTAL
          B16:/F$@SUM(B9.B14)
          /R:C16.H16:RR
          B16:/FI
          C16:/FI
```

Figure 5.8: Spreadsheet Instructions: SALES ANALYSIS (cont.)

We enter the unit sales data for each item into positions B9 through B15. We determine the sales price by multiplying the unit price in the product table by the number of units sold. Thus, to obtain the dollar volume of drills, we write:

```
        C9:/FI +B9*B26
```

We then determine the dollar volume for the other tools with a simple replication:

```
/R:C10.C14:RR
```

Next, we use this calculation to obtain the gross profit figure for each item:

$$\text{Gross Profit} = \text{Sales Price} - \text{Cost}$$
$$= \text{Units Sold}*(\text{Price/Unit} - \text{Cost/Unit})$$

In VisiCalc notation, we write:

```
E9:+B9*(B26−C26)
/R:E10.E14:RRR
```

Next, we find the net profit for each item by subtracting the item's share of fixed expenses from the gross profit. We allocate fixed expenses on a unit basis. Thus, we write:

```
G7:NET PROF
  G9:+E9−(B9/B16*B33)
  /R:G10.G14:RRNN
```

Finally, the report is completed when the percentages are calculated and the columns are added. Thus, to calculate a portion of the items, we write:

```
D7:" %
  D9:100*C9/C16
  /R:D10.D14:RN
A16:TOTAL
  B16:F$@SUM(B9.B14)
  /R:C16.H16:RR
  B16:/FI
  C16:/FI
```

A series of replications completes the calculations.

ADDITIONAL REMARKS

You can use the INSERT ROW command to extend this form so that it can compute any number of items. Using this command assures that all the formulas remain in the correct order.

By reviewing the data shown in this example, you can see that in terms of units sold, drills are the largest seller with 1,000 units sold. However, in terms of percentages, grinders show the best performance results. If you allocate expenses on a units sold basis, the sanders and grinders have made the largest contribution to profit.

PLOTTING THE DATA

For this example, we will create a pie chart that shows the unit volume sales of each product. To do this, we create a series in the DIF format by writing:

    B9:
    /S#S
    UNIT. DIF
    B14
    C

Figure 5.9 shows a pie chart generated on a Hewlett-Packard 125 computer with the Graphics 125 package using data in the DIF file.

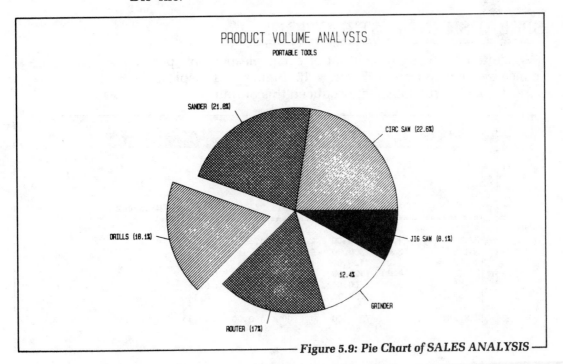

Figure 5.9: Pie Chart of SALES ANALYSIS

SALESPERSON ANALYSIS

We will now examine a simple, but important application of the VisiCalc program. We will prepare a report that analyzes the sales performance of a group of sales people.

APPLICATION EXAMPLE

Let's assume that a company has geographically divided its sales territory into six zones. You have determined the sales potential of each zone and are accumulating performance data on each salesperson. You plan to prepare a report that summarizes these sales figures. To do this, you need to calculate the percentage of overall sales contributed by each salesperson, with the ratio when compared with those of the total market.

SPREADSHEET INSTRUCTIONS

A printout showing the output of each salesperson's performance by zone appears in Figure 5.10. Figure 5.11 displays the spreadsheet instructions that produced this output.

```
      A          B        C         D        E      F       G
                             MYCO INC.
                  415 WEST HARRISON STREET
                  JACKSON   CALIF.   94223

                  SALESPEOPLE ANALYSIS BY ZONE        MAR. 1982
  ====================================================================
7  SALESPERSON  ZONE     SIZE      SALES     %     RATIO
8  BROWN        1.00   1000.00    200.00   17.01   0.20
9  SMITH        2.00   1300.00    300.00   25.51   0.23
10 JONES        3.00   1100.00    170.00   14.46   0.15
11 GREEN        4.00   1500.00    176.00   14.97   0.12
12 ADAMS        5.00   1200.00    190.00   16.16   0.16
13 LARSON       6.00   1250.00    140.00   11.90   0.11
14
15 COMPANY             7350.00   1176.00   100.00   0.16
```

Figure 5.10: SALESPEOPLE ANALYSIS

```
/CY
/GF$
/SL MASTER.VC
C5:SALESPEOP        D5:LE ANALYS      E5:IS BY ZONE      F5:E
G5:MAR. 1982
A7:/FR
/R:B7.F7
A7:SALESPERS        B7:/FL ON ZONE    C7:SIZE            D7:SALES
   E7:" %
      E8:100*D8/D15
      /R:E9.E13:RN
   F7:RATIO
      F8:+D8/C8
      /R:F9.F13:RR
   A15:COMPANY
      C15:@SUM(C8.C13)
      /R:D15.E15:RR
      F15:+D15/C15
```

────── *Figure 5.11: Spreadsheet Instructions: SALESPEOPLE ANALYSIS* ──────

We enter into columns C and D, the data that specifies the market size and the actual sales volume. We write the column totals as:

```
C15:@SUM(C8.C13)
/R:D15.E15:RR
```

We obtain the figures for each salesperson's percentage of total sales by specifying:

```
E8:100*D8/D15
/R:E9.E13:RN
```

We compute the ratio of each salesperson's sales to the sales potential of the zone by writing:

```
F8:+D8/C8
/R:F9.F13:RR
```

To obtain the company's ratio, we write:

```
F15:+D15/C15
```

As shown in Figure 5.10, the highest percentage of sales was obtained by Smith; however, by looking at the ratios, we can also see that she has the highest sales ratio.

ADDITIONAL REMARKS

You can easily modify this report to add a new feature and obtain information that can be used to compare each salesperson's ratio with the company's ratio. You can do this by adding the following formula:

```
G7:/FR SALES/CO
G8: + F8/F15
/R:G9.G13:RN
```

Figure 5.12 shows the reprinted report.

	A	B	C	D	E	F	G
1				MYCO INC.			
2			415 WEST HARRISON STREET				
3			JACKSON	CALIF.	94223		
4							
5			SALESPEOPLE ANALYSIS BY ZONE				MAR. 1982
6	==						
7	SALESPERSON	ZONE	SIZE	SALES	%	RATIO	SALES/CO
8	BROWN	1.00	1000.00	200.00	17.01	0.20	1.25
9	SMITH	2.00	1300.00	300.00	25.51	0.23	1.44
10	JONES	3.00	1100.00	170.00	14.46	0.15	.96
11	GREEN	4.00	1500.00	176.00	14.97	0.12	.73
12	ADAMS	5.00	1200.00	190.00	16.16	0.16	.98
13	LARSON	6.00	1250.00	140.00	11.90	0.11	.70
14							
15	COMPANY		7350.00	1176.00	100.00	0.16	

Figure 5.12: SALESPEOPLE ANALYSIS WITH RATIO

PLOTTING THE DATA

We will now plot this data on a comparative bar chart. We will compare each salesperson's percentage of compound sales with his or her zone penetration ratio. To do this, we create two series in DIF. We create the ratio series by writing:

```
F8:
/S#S
RATIO.DIF
F13
C
```

We follow the same procedure to create the percentage series. Next, we plot the data. Figure 5.13 shows a bar chart that we have created on a Hewlett-Packard 125 computer using the Graphics 125 package and the DIF series.

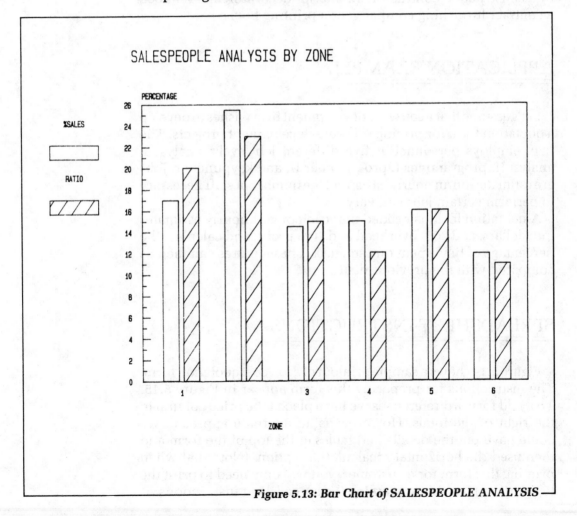

Figure 5.13: Bar Chart of SALESPEOPLE ANALYSIS

QUOTATION PREPARATION

Many businesses use standarized forms for preparing job-cost quotations. If they are well-designed, these forms can be extremely useful tools. In this example we will prepare a quotation form for a custom software company. (*Note:* this form could also be used by a construction contractor, an interior decorator, an architect, a contract furnishing company, or a printing house.)

APPLICATION EXAMPLE

Let's assume that a software development firm wishes to develop a quotation form for pricing software development projects. The firm employs personnel at five different job levels: analyst I, analyst II, programmer I, programmer II, and keypuncher. Jobs are estimated on an hourly basis, and the number of staff necessary to perform certain jobs can vary.

A quotation form is needed that can convert hourly estimates into dollars, add 20% overhead and 10% profit, and calculate the percentage of time spent on each task. These figures can then be compared with the previous data.

SPREADSHEET INSTRUCTIONS

Figure 5.14 shows a sample printout of a job-cost quotation form. The instructions for preparing this form appear in Figure 5.15. To avoid forward references we have placed the price column to the right of the totals. However, as an alternate approach we could have put the details and tables at the top of the form and then used the horizontal recalculation option. (Note that when printing this form for a customer, you will only need to print the top portion.) Let's now examine the spreadsheet instructions.

```
        A          B          C          D          E          F          G
 1                             MYCO INC.
 2                 415 WEST HARRISON STREET
 3                 JACKSON   CALIF.   94223
 4
 5                     QUOTATION                        JAN. 1982
 6  ================================================================
 7                 ITEM                                          PRICE
 8                 ANALYZE  REQTS                                3260
 9                 SPECIFICATION                                 2900
10                 DESIGN                                        2670
11                 CODING                                        1400
12                 CHECKOUT                                      2120
13                 TEST                                          3260
14                 DOCUMENTATION                                 2040
15
16                 KEYPUNCH                                       700
17                 COMPUTER TIME                                68750
18
19                 TOTAL                                        87100
20
21                 OVERHEAD                                     17420
22                 PROFIT                                        8710
23
24                 TOTAL                                       113230
25
26                         DETAIL   (HOURS)
27                 A1         A2         P1         P2      TOTAL       %
28  ANALYSIS       80        120         20          0       220      14
29  SPEC           60         80         40         40       220      14
30  DESIGN         20         30        130         60       240      16
31  CODING          0          0         40        120       160      11
32  CHECK           0         20         80        120       220      14
33  TEST           40         60        100         80       280      18
34  DOC            20         40         60         60       180      12
35                                               =========
36  KEYPUNCH      100                               1520
37  COMP TIME     250
38          RATE       TABLE
39  A1             17
40  A2             14
41  P1             11
42  P2              8
43  KP              7
44  COMP TIME     275
```

Figure 5.14: QUOTATION PREPARATION

```
/CY
/SL MASTER.VC
/GFI
```

Figure 5.15:
Spreadsheet Instruction: QUOTATION PREPARATION (continues)

```
            D5:QUOTATION    G5:JAN. 1982
            C7:ITEM
            C8:ANALYZE      D8:REQTS
            C9:SPECIFICA    D9:TION
            C10:DESIGN
            C11:CODING
            C12:CHECKOUT
            C13:TEST
            C14:DOCUMENTA   D14:TION
            G7:/FR PRICE
              G8:(B28*B39)+(C28*B40)+(D28*B41)+(E28*B42)
              /R:G9.G14:RN RN RN RN
            C16:KEYPUNCH
              G16:+B36*B43
            C17:COMPUTER    D17:TIME
              G17:+B37*B44
            C19:TOTAL
              G19:@SUM(G8.G17)
            C21:OVERHEAD
              G21: .2*G19
            C22:PROFIT
              G22: .1*G19
            C24:TOTAL
              G24:@SUM(G19.G22)
            D26:DETAIL       E26:"(HOURS)
            A27:/FR
            /R:B27.G27
            B27:A1           C27:A2          D27:P1          E27:P2
            A28:ANALYSIS
            A29:SPEC
            A30:DESIGN
            A31:CODING
            A32:CHECK
            A33:TEST
            A34:DOC
            A36:KEYPUNCH
```

*Figure 5.15: Spreadsheet Instruction: **QUOTATION PREPARATION** (continues)*

```
    A37:COMP TIME
      F27:TOTAL
        F28:@SUM(B28.E28)
        /R:F29.F34:RR
      F35:/—=
        F36:@SUM(F28.F34)
      G27:" %
        G28:100*F28/F36
        /R:G29.G34:RN
B38:RATE              C38:TABLE
  A39:A1             A40:A2           A41:P1           A42:P2
  A43:KP             A44:COMP TIME
```

Figure 5.15: Spreadsheet Instructions: QUOTATION PREPARATION (cont.)

For this example we first enter the estimated hours into the "DETAIL" portion of the form. We then total the hours and compute the percentage of total time required by each task. We write this as:

```
F27:TOTAL
  F28:@SUM(B28.E28)
  /R:F29.F34:RR
  F36:@SUM(F28.F34)
 G27:"%
  G28:100*F28/F36
  /R:G29.G34:RN
```

Next, we extend the prices by adding the hours—after they have been multiplied by the hourly rate for each category. For example, to calculate the line labeled "analyze requirements," we write:

```
G8:(B28*B39)+(C28*B40)+(D28*B41)+(E28*B42)
/R:G9.G14:RN RN RN RN
```

This expression yields the total cost of labor for all job classifications performing this particular task. We then replicate the formula for the other tasks.

Next, we add the keypunch and computer time to the above labor figures to obtain the direct projected cost. Thus, we write:

```
C16:KEYPUNCH
    G16: +B36*B43
C17:COMPUTER D17:TIME
    G17: +B37*B44
C19:TOTAL
    G19:@SUM(G8.G17)
```

We complete the quotation by calculating the overhead and profit; we then add these figures to obtain a grand total:

```
C21:OVERHEAD
    G21: .2*G19
C22:PROFIT
    G22: .1*G19
C24:TOTAL
    G24:@SUM(G19.G22)
```

SALES FORECAST— PRICING MODEL

The next several examples explore the use of mathematical models in the preparation of sales forecasts. The VisiCalc program has many built-in functions that are useful when preparing these models. In the first example we will make projections of the future profits of a company based on an exponential supply-demand curve.

APPLICATION EXAMPLE

A gasoline dealer must analyze his sales data. He knows that sales, as a function of price, can be represented by the equation:

$$G = K*(e^\wedge - (a*x))$$

where
$$G = \text{gallons per month}$$
$$K = \text{constant}$$
$$a = \text{constant}$$
$$x = \text{dollars per gallon}$$

The dealer's cost of gasoline is 80% of the sales price. His fixed costs are currently $30,000 per month and have been increasing by .75% per month. The price of gasoline is expected to rise 12% per year. The dealer wishes to prepare a sales and income forecast for the next twelve months.

SPREADSHEET INSTRUCTIONS

A printout of a sales forecast appears in Figure 5.16. The spreadsheet instructions for this example are shown in Figure 5.17.

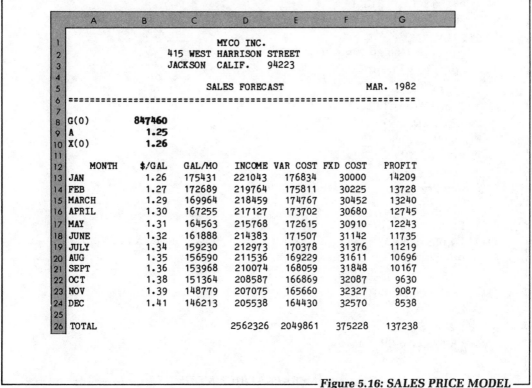

	A	B	C	D	E	F	G
1				MYCO INC.			
2			415 WEST HARRISON STREET				
3			JACKSON CALIF. 94223				
4							
5				SALES FORECAST		MAR. 1982	
6	==						
7							
8	G(0)	847460					
9	A	1.25					
10	X(0)	1.26					
11							
12	MONTH	$/GAL	GAL/MO	INCOME	VAR COST	FXD COST	PROFIT
13	JAN	1.26	175431	221043	176834	30000	14209
14	FEB	1.27	172689	219764	175811	30225	13728
15	MARCH	1.29	169964	218459	174767	30452	13240
16	APRIL	1.30	167255	217127	173702	30680	12745
17	MAY	1.31	164563	215768	172615	30910	12243
18	JUNE	1.32	161888	214383	171507	31142	11735
19	JULY	1.34	159230	212973	170378	31376	11219
20	AUG	1.35	156590	211536	169229	31611	10696
21	SEPT	1.36	153968	210074	168059	31848	10167
22	OCT	1.38	151364	208587	166869	32087	9630
23	NOV	1.39	148779	207075	165660	32327	9087
24	DEC	1.41	146213	205538	164430	32570	8538
25							
26	TOTAL			2562326	2049861	375228	137238

Figure 5.16: SALES PRICE MODEL

```
/CY
/SL MASTER.VC
/GFI
C5:/FR SA           D5:LES FOREC      E5:AST              G5:MAR. 1982
A8:G(0)
A9:A
   B9:/FG B10:/F$
A10:X(0)
A12:/FR
/R:B12.G12
A12:MONTH
   A13:JAN          A14:FEB           A15:MARCH           A16:APRIL
   A17:MAY          A18:JUNE          A19:JULY            A20:AUG
   A21:SEPT         A22:OCT           A23:NOV             A24:DEC
B12:" $/GAL
   B13:/F$ +B10
   B14:/F$ 1.01*B13
   /R:B15.B24:R
C12:GAL/MO
   C13:+B8*@EXP(−B9*B13)
   /R:C14.C24:NNR
D12:INCOME
   D13:+B13*C13
   /R:D14.D24:RR
E12:VAR COST
   E13: .8*D13
   /R:E14.E24:R
F12:FXD COST
   F13:30000
   F14:(1+.0075)*F13
   /R:F15.F24:R
G12:PROFIT
   G13:+D13−E13−F13
   /R:G14.G24:RRR
A26:TOTAL
   D26:@SUM(D13.D24)
   /R:E26.G26:RR
```

Figure 5.17: Spreadsheet Instructions: SALES PRICE MODEL

We begin by calculating the price of gasoline per month. The first month is given as X(0). Therefore, we write:

    B13:/F$ +B10

The price of gas is expected to rise 1% per month. To calculate the price per month, we write:

    B14:/F$ 1.01*B13
    /R:B15.B24:R

Recall that we can obtain the gallonage per month by using the equation:

$$G = K * (e^\wedge - (a * x))$$

In VisiCalc notation, we write the January gallonage as:

    C13:+B8*@EXP(−B9*B13)

We then replicate this formula for the balance of the months by writing:

    /R:C14.C24:NNR

We can now determine the monthly income by multiplying the price per gallon by the gallons per month:

    D13:+B13*C13
    /R:D14.D24:RR

The variable cost is 80% of the sales volume. This is calculated and replicated by writing:

    E13:.8*D13
    /R:E14.E24:R

The fixed cost is $30,000 and is rising at .75% per month. We express this as:

    F13:30000
    F14:(1+.0075)*F13
    /R:F15.F24:R

Finally, we compute the profit per month by subtracting the costs from the income:

    G13:+D13−E13−F13
    /R:G14.G24:RRR

As we can see in Figure 5.16, the drop in gallonage is causing a small loss in revenue, and a rather large loss in profit.

PLOTTING THE DATA

We will now prepare a computer-generated graph to show the effect of price per gallon on sales volume. We will use the DIF file format to save two series—price per gallon and gallons per month. The save instructions are:

    B12:
    /S#S
    PRICE.DIF
    B23
    C

and

    C12:
    /S#S
    GAL.DIF
    C23
    C

Figure 5.18 shows examples of these two series, which have been plotted on an Apple Silentype™ printer using the VisiPlot program.

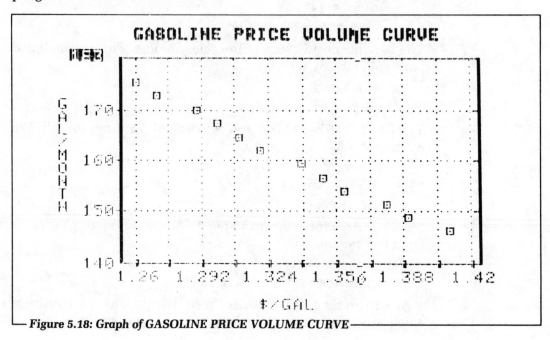

Figure 5.18: Graph of GASOLINE PRICE VOLUME CURVE

SALES FORECAST—MATURITY CURVE

In this example, we will investigate the use of a mathematical model for preparing a sales forecast for a new product. We will select an "S" curve model for this example.

APPLICATION EXAMPLE

In the sales growth curve shown in Figure 5.19, the new product was put on the market at T0. Sales increased very slowly during the introductory phase and then began to accelerate as the product became more popular. Eventually at T2, sales growth began to slow as the market began to reach saturation. At T3, growth had slowed substantially.

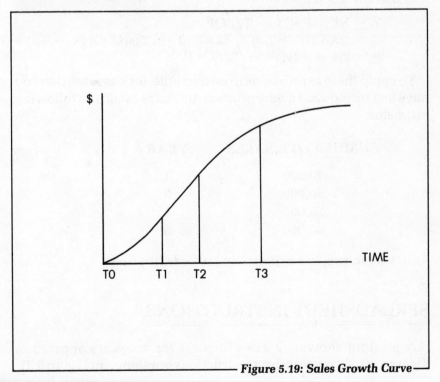

Figure 5.19: Sales Growth Curve

One way of modeling this growth pattern is to break the curve into two parts: accelerating sales and decelerating sales:

FOR T < T2
$Y = A*(X^B)$

where

Y = units sold
X = time
A & B are constants

If we predict the unit sales at T1 and T2 as S1 and S2, respectively, we have:

$S1 = A*(T1^B)$
$S2 = A*(T2^B)$

and we can show that:

$B = (LOG\ S1 - LOG\ S2)/(LOG\ T1 - LOG\ T2)$
$A = S1/(T1^B)$

and that for T > T2

$Y - S2 = P*((X - T2)^Q)$
$Q = (LOG(S4 - S2) - LOG(S3 - S2))/(LOG(T4 - T2) - LOG(T3 - T2))$
$P = (S4 - S2)/(T4 - T2)^Q*P$

To apply these expressions to an example, let's assume that you have just introduced a new product and have made the following estimates:

CUMULATIVE SALES	YEAR
10,000	1
50,000	3
75,000	4
90,000	5

You wish to prepare a quarterly six-year forecast.

SPREADSHEET INSTRUCTIONS

A printout showing a sales forecast for six years appears in Figure 5.20. The spreadsheet instructions are shown in Figure 5.21.

```
       A          B          C          D          E          F          G
 1                              MYCO INC.
 2                     415 WEST HARRISON STREET
 3                     JACKSON  CALIF.   94223
 4
 5                         SALES FORECAST              JUNE 1982
 6  ================================================================
 7                    ASSUMPTIONS
 8          CUM SALES      YEAR
 9          10000.00       1.00
10          50000.00       3.00
11          75000.00       4.00
12          90000.00       5.00
13
14          0<T<3     S=A(T^B)
15          3<T<6     S=P*((T-T2)^Q)+S2
16
17     PARAM     VALUE       LOG
18  S1          10000.00     4.00
19  S2          50000.00     4.70
20  S3          75000.00     4.88
21  S4          90000.00     4.95
22  T1              1.00     0.00
23  T2              3.00     0.48
24  T3              4.00     0.60
25  T4              5.00     0.70
26  S3-S2       25000.00     4.40
27  S4-S2       40000.00     4.60
28  T4-T2           2.00     0.30
29  T3-T2           1.00     0.00
30                 B         1.46
31                 A     10000.00
32                 Q         0.68
33                 P     25000.00
34
35                    SALES (UNITS)
36     YEAR         1         2         3         4         5         6
37  SALES        10000     27606     50000     75000     90000    102658
```

Figure 5.20: SALES FORECAST—MATURITY CURVE

```
/CY
/SL MASTER.VC
/GF$
/GOR
C5:/FR SAL        D5:ES FORECA      E5:ST              G5:JUNE 1982
C7:ASSUMPTIO      D7:NS
  B8:CUM SALES      C8:/FR YEAR
  B14:"0<T<3        C14:S=A*(T^B)
```

Figure 5.21: Spreadsheet Instructions: SALES FORECAST—MATURITY CURVE

```
      B15:"3<T<6        C15:S=P*((T−T        D15:"2)^Q)+S2
A17:/FR
/R:B17.C17
A17:PARAM          B17:VALUE              C17:LOG
   A18:S1
   B18:+B9
   /R:B19.B21:R
   C18:@LOG10(B18)
   /R:C19.C29:R
   A19:S2
   A20:S3
   A21:S4
   A22:T1
   B22:+C9
   /R:B23.B25:R
   A23:T2
   A24:T3
   A25:T4
   A26:S3−S2        B26:+B20−B19
   A27:S4−S2        B27:+B21−B19
   A28:T4−T2        B28:+B25−B23
   A29:T3−T2        B29:+B24−B23
   B30:/FR B
      C30:(C18−C19)/(C22−C23)
   B31:/FR A
      C31:+B18/(B22^C30)
   B32:/FR Q
      C32:(C27−C26)/(C28−C29)
   B33:/FR P
      C33:+B26/(B29^C32)
   C35:SALES (UN     D35:ITS)
A36:/FR
/R:B36.G36
A36:YEAR
   B36:1            C36:2            D36:3
   E36:4            F36:5            G36:6
```

Figure 5.21: Spreadsheet Instructions: SALES FORECAST—MATURITY CURVE (continues)

```
A37:SALES
    B37:/FI +C31*(B36^C30)
    /R:C37.D37:NRN
    E37:/FI +C33*((E36-B23)^C32)+B19
    /R:F37.G37:NRNNN
```

Figure 5.21: Spreadsheet Instructions: SALES FORECAST—MATURITY CURVE (cont.)

For this example we have provided a parameter table at the beginning of the spreadsheet. This table includes the projected cumulative rates for various years. Because they are grouped in a table, the growth estimates can be easily changed, and we can obtain new forecasts quickly.

Since the formulas that we are using for the curves are fairly complex, we show them in the report. Also, since the computation of the constants is somewhat involved, we calculate and display each constant individually.

When using the curve fitting technique it is a good idea to print the parameters so that they are available for review. For this example we will print the parameters in a second table.

Due to the way we have laid out the form we must perform the recalculations horizontally. The command

    /GOR

causes the VisiCalc program to compute in row, rather than column, order.

In the spreadsheet instructions, to copy the parameters from Table 1 to Table 2, we write:

    B18:+B9
    /R:B19.B21:R
    B22:+C9
    /R:B23.B25:R

We use the quantities S3−S2, S4−S2, T4−T2, and T3−T2 to determine the coefficients of the equations. We add them to the 2nd table by writing:

    B26:+B20−B19
    B27:+B21−B19
    B28:+B25−B23
    B29:+B24−B23

The logarithms to the base ten are required for all values in the second table. To generate them, we write:

    C18:@LOG10(B18)
    /R:C19.C29:R

We are now ready to complete the four coefficients, A,B,P, and Q, which are derived from the formulas given previously:

    B30:/FR B
        C30:(C18−C19)/(C22−C23)
    B31:/FR A
        C31:+B18/(B22^C30)
    B32:/FR Q
        C32:(C27−C26)/(C28−C29)
    B33:/FR P
        C33:+B26/(B29^C32)

We now know the coefficients for the two curves, and we can complete the forecast. For the first three years, we use the first form of the equation. We repeat the equation:

$$S = A*(T^B)$$

Thus, in VisiCalc notation, we write:

    B37:/FI +C31*(B36^C30)
    /R:C37.D37:NRN

For the second three years, we compute:

$$S = P*((T - T2)^Q) + S2$$

In VisiCalc notation, we write:

    E37:/FI +C33*((E36−B23)^C32)+B19
    /R:F37.G37NRNNN

ADDITIONAL REMARKS

The expression for sales at any point in time represents the yearly rate at that given time. Thus, the figures in the tables represent the number of units that *should* be sold during that time period. It is possible to calculate the number of units that are forecast to be sold in an individual quarter by subtracting the number forecast at the beginning of the quarter from the number realized at the end. For example, you can obtain a forecast for the sixth quarter by writing:

    A41: Q6
        B41:C31*(6/4^C30)
    A42: Q5
        B42:C31*(5/4^C30)
    A43: Q6−Q5
        B43:+A41−A42

SALES FORECAST— LINEAR REGRESSION

In previous forecasting examples, we have made several assumptions regarding future growth. For example, we have based projections on an assumed sales growth rate of 10%; we have also fit an assumed curve shape through two points in order to predict growth. In this example we will use linear regression to fit the best straight line through the historical data. (*Note:* we discuss the curvilinear regression technique in detail in Chapter 6.)

APPLICATION EXAMPLE

You have recorded eight quarters of deseasonalized sales data and you plan to use it to forecast sales for the next four quarters.

SPREADSHEET INSTRUCTIONS

We can use the equation

$$Y = MX + B$$

to represent a straight line, where M determines the slope and B determines the origin of the line. A linear regression will fit a straight line through the actual data by minimizing the error between the line and the data. This is represented by the following equation:

$$M = SUM(XI*YI) - (SUM(X)*SUM(Y)/N)/(SUM(X^2)$$
$$- SUM(X)^2/N)$$
$$B = YAV - M*XAV$$

We can set up a linear regression on a VisiCalc spreadsheet if we have the following data:

1. the actual historical data, x and y

2. the sum of the products of x and y for each year

3. the sum of all the x's and y's

4. the square of the sum of the x's

5. the sum of the squares of the individual x's

The printout for the sales forecast for this example appears in Figure 5.22. This figure displays the right quarters of deseasonalized data. The spreadsheet instructions appear in Figure 5.23.

	A	B	C	D	E	F	G
1				MYCO INC.			
2			415 WEST HARRISON STREET				
3			JACKSON CALIF. 94223				
4							
5			SALES FORECAST			MAR. 1982	
6	==						
7							
8	QUART(X)	SALES(Y)	X^2	Y^2	X*Y		
9	1	100	1	10000	100		
10	2	103	4	10609	206		
11	3	108	9	11664	324		
12	4	116	16	13456	464		
13	5	120	25	14400	600		
14	6	126	36	15876	756		
15	7	129	49	16641	903		
16	8	136	64	18496	1088		
17	--						
18	36	938	204	111142	4441		
19							
20	N	8					
21	YAV	117					
22	XAV	5					
23	E	220					
24	F	42					
25	M	5					
26	B	94					
27	G	1162					
28	R	.9921484					
29							
30	FORECAST						
31	QUARTER	SALES					
32	9	140.82					
33	10	146.06					
34	11	151.30					
35	12	156.54					

Figure 5.22: SALES FORECAST—LINEAR REGRESSION

```
/CY
/SL MASTER.VC
/GOR
/GFI
C5:/FR    SAL         D5:ES FORECA       E5:ST              G5:MAR 1982
A8:/FR
/R:B8.E8
A8:QUART(X)       B8:SALES(Y)
A17:/ — —
/R:B17.E17
C8:X^2
   C9:+A9^2
   /R:C10.C16:R
D8:Y^2
   D9:+B9^2
   /R:D10.D16:R
E8:X*Y
   E9:+A9*B9
   /R:E10.E16:RR
A18:@SUM(A9.A16)
/R:B18.E18:RR
A20:/FR
/R:A21.A28
A20:N
   B20:@COUNT(A9.A16)
A21:YAV
   B21:@AVE(B9.B16)
A22:XAV
   B22:@AVE(A9.A16)
A23:E
   B23:+E18—(A18*B18/B20)
A24:F
   B24:+C18—(A18^2/B20)
A25:M
```

Figure 5.23:
Spreadsheet Instructions: SALES FORECAST—LINEAR REGRESSION (continues)

```
            B25: +B23/B24
        A26:B
            B26: +B21 — (B22*B25)
        A27:G
            B27: +D18 — (B18^2/B20)
        A28:R
            B28:/FG +B23^2/(B24*B27)
        A30:FORECAST
    A31:/FR QUARTER  B31:/FR SALES
    A32:9           A33:10          A34:11          A35:12
            B32:/F$ +A32*B25+B26
            /R:B33.B35:RNN
```

Figure 5.23: Spreadsheet Instructions: SALES FORECAST—LINEAR REGRESSION (cont.)

We devote the first table in the form to calculating the values that we need to determine the coefficients of the equations. As in the previous example, the spreadsheet layout requires calculation in row order. We accomplish this by writing:

```
/GOR
```

Next we calculate the value needed to determine M & B. We square the individual x's by writing:

```
C9: +A9^2
/R:C10.C16:R
```

Likewise, we square the y's by writing:

```
D9: +B9^2
/R:D10.D16:R
```

We then calculate the individual products:

```
E9: +A9*B9
/R:E10.E16:RR
```

Next, we calculate the sum of each column:

```
A18: @SUM(A9.A16)
/R:B18.E18:RR
```

Then, we use the VisiCalc COUNT function to obtain the number of data points, N:

A20:N
   B20:@COUNT(A9.A16)

The COUNT function provides the number of non-zero entries within its parameter range.

Next, we average the historical data:

B21:@AVE(B9.B16)
B22:@AVE(A9.A16)

To find M we must compute E and F:

$$E = +SUM(X*Y) - (SUM(X)SUM(Y)/N)$$

in VisiCalc notation, we write:

B23:+E18−(A18*B18/B20)

To compute

$$F = SUM(X^2) - (SUM(X))^2/N$$

in VisiCalc notation, we write:

B24:+C18−(A18^2/B20)

To determine

$$M = E/F$$

we write:

B25:+B23/B24

To calculate

$$B = YAV - M*XAV$$

in VisiCalc notation, we write:

B26:+B21−(B22*B25)

Note that in almost all of the previous formulas, parentheses must appear in the equation; otherwise, an incorrect result will occur.

Another important parameter that we must compute is the correlation coefficient, R. This coefficient reveals how "well" the line fits the data. If R is equal to 1, the fit is perfect; if it is equal to 0, there is no fit. For example:

$$R = E^2/(FG)$$

where

$$G = SUM(Y^2) - (SUM(Y)^2/N)$$

Thus, in VisCalc notation, we write:

```
B27: +D18 − (B18^2/B20)
B28:/FG  +B23^2/(B24∗B27)
```

In this example, R equals .992. We conclude that the straight line is a good fit.

Finally, we forecast sales by computing

$$Y = M * X + B$$

In VisiCalc notation, we write:

```
B32:/F$  +A32∗B25+B26
/R:B33.B35:RNN
```

SUMMARY

In this chapter, we have explored the use of the VisiCalc program as a sales forecasting and analysis tool. We have developed sample forecasting models using compound growth and more complex mathematical models. We have prepared spreadsheets that can help analyze the contributions of product and sales personnel. In addition, we have demonstrated the use of these spreadsheets as inputs to graphics programs.

6
MANUFACTURING

Bill of Materials   Job Log   Learning Curve Analysis
Inventory Forecast   Quality Control
Quality Control Analysis   Hiring Plan

OVERVIEW

In this chapter we will explore a variety of VisiCalc applications in the manufacturing field. As before, these examples can be used as presented, or modified to meet individual company requirements.

In the first example we will prepare a simple record-keeping statement: a bill of materials. This bill can be used to record information on part numbers, item descriptions, and costs.

In the next example we will create a job control log. We can use this log to prepare an estimate of the time necessary to complete a job.

In manufacturing situations it is common to use learning curve analyses to make estimates on future production times based on sample runs. In the third example we will use the VisiCalc program to perform learning curve estimates.

In the fourth example we will develop a spreadsheet that can be used to forecast inventory requirements in terms of projected sales. The method we will use in this example is based on the linear regression analysis technique developed in Chapter 5, but in this example we will use a non-linear forecasting tool.

The next example illustrates the use of the VisiCalc program for maintaining quality control. In this example we will demonstrate a method for calculating the standard deviation of a quantity of samples.

Finally, we will develop a hiring plan for a rapidly growing manufacturing concern. This plan will include sales data, forecasts, production time estimates, and available manpower.

BILL OF MATERIALS

In this example we will use the VisiCalc program to create a bill of materials for a manufacturing firm. Such bills are normally required for implementing purchasing, inventory, production control, assembly, and engineering projects.

APPLICATION EXAMPLE

Let's assume that you plan to use the VisiCalc program to generate a spreadsheet for a bill of materials, to keep track of the following items: part number, item number, item description, quantity used, and price per unit. In addition, you plan to extend the price list to yield row and column totals.

SPREADSHEET INSTRUCTIONS

Figure 6.1 shows a sample bill for a pressure transducer. The spreadsheet instructions appear in Figure 6.2. They are quite straightforward, so we will provide little discussion.

```
        A        B        C        D        E        F        G
 1                        MYCO INC.
 2              415 WEST HARRISON STREET
 3              JACKSON  CALIF.   94223
 4
 5                   BILL OF MATERIALS          JAN. 1982
 6
 7                   PRESSURE TRANSDUCER
 8  ===================================================================
 9  ITEM NO.      PN  DESCRIPTION      QUANTITY  PRICE/U     TOTAL
10         1    12311  DIAPHRAGM              1     1.25      1.25
11         2    11414  STRAIN  GAUGE          1     4.75      4.75
12         3    11415  CLAMP                  2     0.75      1.50
13         4    12131  O RING                 2     0.34      0.68
14         5    12365  HOUSING                1    12.50     12.50
15         6    11634  FITTING                2     0.95      1.90
16         7    12100  CONNECTOR              1     3.00      3.00
17         8    12694  END CAP                1     2.50      2.50
18                                                            0.00
19                                                            0.00
20                                                            0.00
21                                                            0.00
22                                                            0.00
23                                                            0.00
24                                                            0.00
25                                                            0.00
26                                                            0.00
27                                                            0.00
28                                                            0.00
29                                                            0.00
30                                                            0.00
31                                                            0.00
32                                                            0.00
33  ----------------------------------------------------------------
34                                        TOTAL              28.08
```

Figure 6.1: BILL OF MATERIALS

```
/CY
/SL MASTER.VC
C5:/FR  BIL        D5:L OF MATE      E5:RIALS          G5:JAN. 1982
   C6:/IR /IR
   C7:/FR   PRESS      D7:URE TRANS      E7:DUCER
A9:/FR
/R:B9.G9
A9:ITEM NO.        B9:PN             C9:DESCRIP        D9:/FL TION
E9:QUANTITY        F9:PRICE/U
F10:/F$
```

Figure 6.2: Spreadsheet Instructions: BILL OF MATERIALS (continues)

```
/R:F11.F32
G9:TOTAL
    G10:/F$ +E10*F10
    /R:G11.G32:RR
A33:/ — —
/R:B33.G33
E34:TOTAL
    G34:@SUM(G10.G32)
```

Figure 6.2: Spreadsheet Instructions: BILL OF MATERIALS (cont.)

As usual, we begin by loading the master form into the computer memory. We then extend the title to include the name of the part. Next, we print the title just above the dotted line provided by the master form. We begin the actual instruction specification at coordinate A9.

On the spreadsheet we calculate prices by multiplying the unit price by the quantity needed. Thus, we write:

```
G9:TOTAL
    G10:/F$ +E10*F10
    /R:G11.G32:RR
```

The total price for all items on the bill is simply the total of the extended price column. We write this as:

```
E34:TOTAL
    G34:@SUM(G10.G32)
```

ADDITIONAL REMARKS

You can extend this spreadsheet to include additional items by using the INSERT ROW command. This command will preserve the formulas used previously.

JOB LOG

An essential part of production control is the logging of jobs as they arrive in a department. In this example we will create a job control log to monitor the flow of work for a stereo service shop. We will design the log so that it can be used to analyze job backlogs, as well as to estimate the calendar time needed to turn a job around.

APPLICATION EXAMPLE

Let's assume that you wish to design a job control log and plan to record the following information: the date a job is received, the job control number, the customer's name, a description of the job, the estimated time for completing the job, and the amount of time expended on the job so far. In addition, you wish to record available shop hours and job backlogs to date, and you want to compute and display the calendar days needed to complete the job.

SPREADSHEET INSTRUCTIONS

Figure 6.3 shows an example of a job log printout for a stereo repair shop. Figure 6.4 displays the spreadsheet instructions.

```
             A          B          C          D        E        F        G        H

1                                   MYCO INC.
2                        415 WEST HARRISON STREET
3                        JACKSON  CALIF.   94223
4
5                             INCOMING  JOBS                 JAN. 1982
6   =============================================================================
7   DATE        JOB #     CUST       DESCR      EST HRS   EXP TD    EST TC   STATUS
8   1-4-82      1500      JONES      TUNER         12        8         4     HOLD
9   1-4-82      1501      SMITH      AMP           16        4        12
10  1-5-82      1502      GORDON     MIXER         10        0        10
11  1-5-82      1503      JOSEPH     TUNER         12        0        12
12  1-6-82      1504      ENNIS      DECK          30        0        30
13  1-6-82      1505      NIVEN      RECVR         16        0        16
14  1-6-82      1506      MC HINE    SPEAKER        8        0         8
15  1-6-82      1507      EVANS      CASSETTE       8        0         8
16                                                                    0
17                                                                    0
18                                                                    0
19
20  HOURS       AVAIL                 40
21  BACKLOG                          100
22  DAYS TO     QUOTE                 7.5
```

Figure 6.3: JOB LOG

```
/CY
/SL MASTER.VC
/GOR
C5:/FR   IN          D5:COMING JO    E5:BS              G5:JAN. 1982
E7:/FR
/R:F7.H7
A7:DATE             B7:JOB #
       B8:/FL
       /R:B9.B18
C7:CUST             D7:DESCR
E7:EST HRS          F7:EXP TD
   G7:EST TC
      G8:+E8—F8
      /R:G9.G18:RR
   H7: STATUS
A20:HOURS           B20:AVAIL
A21:BACKLOG
   C21:@SUM(G8.G18)
A22:DAYS TO         B22:QUOTE
   C22:(C21—C20)/8
```

Figure 6.4: Spreadsheet Instructions: JOB LOG

The layout of the spreadsheet is straightforward. In column E we enter the estimated hours for completing the job. In column F we record and update the status of the job. The updating should be done on a routine basis in order to maintain better control over the work in progress. Using these figures, we can estimate the amount of time it will take to complete a job by subtracting these two columns:

```
G7:EST TC
   G8:+E8—F8
   /R:G9.G18:RR
```

At the bottom of the log we record the available shop hours. In this example we use a one-man repair shop; thus, 40 hours per week are available. We express the backlog as the sum of the "EST TC" column. We calculate "DAYS TO QUOTE" by subtracting the available hours from the backlog. In VisiCalc notation we express this procedure as:

```
A20:HOURS          B20:AVAIL
A21:BACKLOG
   C21:@SUM(G8.G18)
A22:DAYS TO        B22:QUOTE
   C22:(C21−C20)/8
```

ADDITIONAL REMARKS

Although we have provided only eight entry positions for this example, you can easily extend the spreadsheet by using the INSERT ROW command.

LEARNING CURVE ANALYSIS

A learning curve is a tool that is often used by planners for estimating future production costs, based on data from pilot runs. We can apply the learning curve technique either by using the historical learning rate of a given organization or by obtaining the actual learning rate by analyzing successive production runs. In this example we will explore the latter method. We will develop a learning curve spreadsheet that allows for the easy estimate of future production costs.

APPLICATION EXAMPLE

Let's assume that a manufacturer is planning a run of items that require five subassemblies. He has made two pilot runs, and from these he has obtained figures for the total number of hours necessary to complete each run. He now wishes to estimate the time and cost required to produce 1,000 units.

SPREADSHEET INSTRUCTIONS

Figure 6.5 shows a sample printout of a manufacturing forecast. The spreadsheet instructions for this example appear in Figure 6.6.

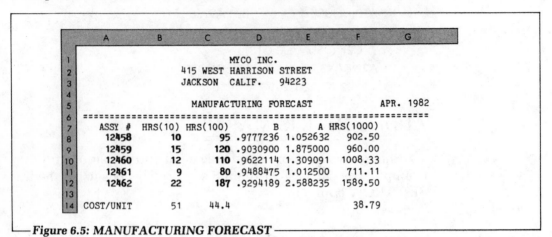

```
        A         B        C           D           E          F        G
1                              MYCO INC.
2                       415 WEST HARRISON STREET
3                       JACKSON  CALIF.   94223
4
5                       MANUFACTURING FORECAST              APR. 1982
6       =========================================================
7       ASSY #  HRS(10) HRS(100)        B         A HRS(1000)
8        12458     10        95  .9777236  1.052632    902.50
9        12459     15       120  .9030900  1.875000    960.00
10       12460     12       110  .9622114  1.309091   1008.33
11       12461      9        80  .9488475  1.012500    711.11
12       12462     22       187  .9294189  2.588235   1589.50
13
14      COST/UNIT  51      44.4                         38.79
```

Figure 6.5: MANUFACTURING FORECAST

```
/CY
/SL MASTER .VC
C5:/FR MANUFAC     D5:TURING FO        E5:RECAST          G5:APR. 1982
   A7:/FR
   /R:B7.G7
   A7:ASSY #       B7:HRS(10)          C7:HRS(100)
   D7:B
      D8:(@LOG10(B8)−@LOG10(C8))/(@LOG10(10)−@LOG10(100))
      /R:D9.D12:RR
   E7:A
      E8:+B8/(10^D8)
      /R:E9.E12:RR
   F7:HRS(1000)
      F8:/F$ +E8*(1000^D8)
      /R:F9.F12:RR
   A14:COST/UNIT
      B14:7.5*@SUM(B8.B12)/10
      C14:7.5*@SUM(C8.C12)/100
      F14:/F$ @SUM(F8.F12)*7.5/1000
```

Figure 6.6: Spreadsheet Instructions: MANUFACTURING FORECAST

The basic equation for a learning curve appears as:

$$Y = A*(X^B)$$

If two sets of X and Y are known, then it is possible to determine the constants, A and B:

$$B = (LOG(Y1) - LOG(Y2))/(LOG(X1) - LOG(X2))$$
$$A = Y1/(X1^B)$$

Our spreadsheet will provide the hours expended (Y) for runs of 10 and 100 units (X). Thus, for each assembly, we write:

A7:ASSY #   B7:HRS(10)   C7:HRS(100)

We enter the data directly into these columns. Next, we compute the constants of the learning curve equation:

D7:B
D8:(@LOG10(B8)−@LOG10(C8))/(@LOG10(10)−@LOG10(100))
/R:D9.D12:RR
E7:A
E8:+B8/(10^D8)
/R:E9.E12:RR

We project the hours needed to manufacture 1,000 of the assemblies by making substitutions in the learning curve equation:

F7:HRS(1000)
F8:/F$ +E8*(1000^D8)
/R:F9.F12:RR

The complete unit that we are manufacturing is built-up from the subassemblies. Therefore, we estimate the total cost for 1,000 units by summing the projected hours for each subassembly and multiplying that figure by the hourly labor rate. For this example we assume that the rate is $7.50 per hour. By simply dividing by the number of units per run, we can compute the price per item in each of the three runs:

A14:COST/UNIT
B14:7.5*@SUM(B8.B12)/10
C14:7.5*@SUM(C8.C12)/100
F14:/F$ @SUM(F8.F12)*7.5/1000

ADDITIONAL REMARKS

As we have discussed previously, we have designed this spreadsheet to handle an item that consists of five subassemblies. It is possible, however, to modify the spreadsheet to account for an arbitrarily large number of subassemblies, or to reduce it to a single item analysis.

If you plan to use the spreadsheet for pilot runs that vary in size, you may want to include a parameter table and modify the formulas accordingly. For example, if you have stored the "NUMBER OF UNITS" at B20 and B21, you may rewrite the formula for A and B as:

```
D7:B
   D8:(@LOG10(B8)−@LOG10(C8))/(@LOG10(B20)−@LOG10(B21))
   /R:D9.D12:RR
E7:A
   E8:+B8/(B20^E8)
   /R:E9.E12:RR
```

You may also want to make other modifications as needed.

INVENTORY FORECAST

In Chapter 5, we presented several forecasting examples. We will now investigate an alternate forecasting method: We will create an inventory forecast that performs a curvilinear regression by a transformation of variables followed by a linear regression.

Studies of manufacturing organizations have shown that inventory often grows at a rate that is slower than the growth of sales. Curvilinear regression is, therefore, an appropriate forecasting method in this situation.

APPLICATION EXAMPLE

Let's assume that you work for a manufacturing firm that has recorded and maintained sales and inventory data for the past seven years. You are asked to prepare a spreadsheet that can be used to estimate inventory requirements for the next three years.

SPREADSHEET INSTRUCTIONS

Figure 6.7 shows a printout of an inventory forecast. The spreadsheet instructions appear in Figure 6.8.

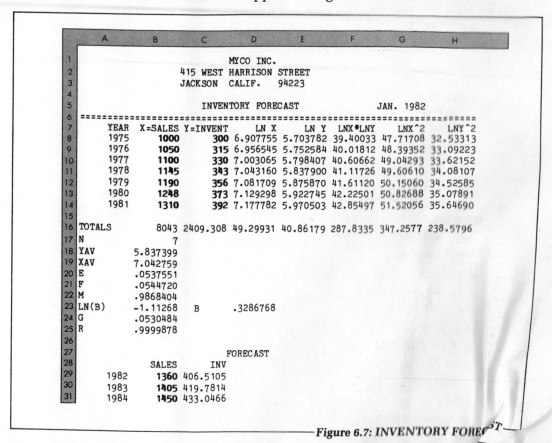

```
              MYCO INC.
         415 WEST HARRISON STREET
         JACKSON   CALIF.   94223

              INVENTORY FORECAST                    JAN. 1982
=================================================================================
      YEAR  X=SALES Y=INVENT     LN X      LN Y   LNX*LNY    LNX^2    LNY^2
      1975    1000      300  6.907755  5.703782  39.40033  47.71708  32.53313
      1976    1050      315  6.956545  5.752584  40.01812  48.39352  33.09223
      1977    1100      330  7.003065  5.798407  40.60662  49.04293  33.62152
      1978    1145      343  7.043160  5.837900  41.11726  49.60610  34.08107
      1979    1190      356  7.081709  5.875870  41.61120  50.15060  34.52585
      1980    1248      373  7.129298  5.922745  42.22501  50.82688  35.07891
      1981    1310      392  7.177782  5.970503  42.85497  51.52056  35.64690

TOTALS        8043 2409.308 49.29931 40.86179 287.8335 347.2577 238.5796
N                7
YAV      5.837399
XAV      7.042759
E         .0537551
F         .0544720
M         .9868404
LN(B)    -1.11268    B     .3286768
G         .0530484
R         .9999878

                    FORECAST
         SALES     INV
   1982   1360 406.5105
   1983   1405 419.7814
   1984   1450 433.0466
```

Figure 6.7: INVENTORY FORECAST

Figure 6.8: Spreadsheet Instructions: INVENTORY FORECAST (continues)

```
A8:1975
A9:1+A8
/R:A10.A14:R
D7:LN X
    D8:@LN(B8)
    /R:D9.D14:R
E7:LN Y
    E8:@LN(C8)
    /R:E9.E14:R
F7:LNX*LNY
    F8:+D8*E8
    /R:F9.F14:RR
G7:LNX^2
    G8:+D8*D8
    /R:G9.G14:RR
H7:LNY^2
    H8:+E8*E8
    /R:H9.H14:RR
A16:TOTALS
    B16:@SUM(B8.B14)
    /R:C16.H16:RR
A17:N
    B17:@COUNT(B8.B14)
A18:YAV
    B18:@AVE(E8.E14)
A19:XAV
    B19:@AVE(D8.D14)
A20:E
    B20:+F16—(D16*E16/B17)
  1:F
    21:+G16—(D16^2/B17)
      A22 B20/B21
        B
          8—(B22*B19)
```

Figure 6.8: Spre   nstructions: INVENTORY FORECAST (continues)

```
              C23:"  B
                 D23:@EXP(B23)
        A24:G
             B24:+H16-(E16^2/B17)
        A25:R
             B25:+B20^2/(B21*B24)
        D27:FORECAST
             B28:/FR SALES      C28:/FR INV
                A29:1982           A30:1983        A31:1984
                C29:+D23*(B29^B22)
                /R:C30.C31:NRN
```

Figure 6.8: Spreadsheet Instructions: INVENTORY FORECAST (cont.)

The method of linear regression (used in previous examples) works when the data being analyzed follow an approximate straight-line relationship. As stated previously, the equation for a straight-line is:

$$Y = MX + B$$

For a given set of data, the linear regression technique determines the coefficients, M and B. The correlation coefficient, R, indicates how well the line fits the data. If the coefficient is "far" from 1, it is not a good fit.

Curvilinear regression tries to fit to the data the equation:

$$Y = B*(X^M)$$

We can use a mathematical transformation to turn this equation into one for a straight-line relationship. To do this, we take the natural logarithms of both sides of the equation:

$$LN(Y) = LN(B) + M*LN(X)$$

We can use the same method that we used in the linear regression example for this spreadsheet, provided that we first take the logarithms of the data. We can directly determine the coefficient M and the logarithm of B. We can also directly compute the correlation coefficient.

Let's now summarize the spreadsheet instructions that we used to set up the forecast. (For additional details, refer to the examples in Chapter 5.)

We begin this example by calculating the logarithms of X and Y.

We then find the product of the logs, and the squares of the logs. To do this, we write:

```
D7:LN X
  D8:@LN(B8)
  /R:D9.D14:R
E7:LN Y
  E8:@LN(C8)
  /R:E9.E14:R
F7:LNX*LNY
  F8:+D8*E8
  /R:F9.F14:RR
G7:LNX^2
  G8:+D8*D8
  /R:G9.G14:RR
H7:LNY^2
  H8:+E8*E8
  /R:H9.H14:RR
```

As before, we need the column totals, the number of entries, and the average of the transformed data. Thus, we write:

```
A16:TOTALS
  B16:@SUM(B8.B14)
  /R:C16.H16:RR
A17:N
  B17:@COUNT(B8.B14)
A18:YAV
  B18:@AVE(E8.E14)
A19:XAV
  B19:@AVE(D8.D14)
```

Using prior terminology, we next calculate E and F and then compute M, G, and R. This time we compute LN(B), rather than B. We must, therefore, transpose back, in order to obtain B:

```
A20:E
  B20:+F16-(D16*E16/B17)
A21:F
  B21:+G16-(D16^2/B17)
A22:M
  B22:+B20/B21
A23:LN(B)
```

B23: +B18—(B22*B19)

    C23:"   B

        D23:@EXP(B23)

A24:G

    B24: +H16—(E16^2/B17)

A25:R

    B25: +B20^2/(B21*B24)

Next, we make the inventory forecast using the relationship

$$Y = B*(X^M)$$

Thus, we write:

    C29: +D23*(B29^B22)

    /R:C30.C31:NRN

and the forecast is completed.

QUALITY CONTROL

This example reviews the methodology necessary to develop a VisiCalc spreadsheet that will calculate the mean and standard deviation of a series of measurements. By assuring that the standard deviation is within an acceptable limit, we can maintain that a sample product batch has parameters that are also acceptable.

APPLICATION EXAMPLE

To assure product quality control in your company, you have requested that a series of weight measurements be taken of random product packages as they proceed down a production line. You want to design a form on which this information can be recorded, and you wish to calculate the standard deviation of the weights, as well as the average, minimum, and maximum weight.

SPREADSHEET INSTRUCTIONS

Figure 6.9 shows a sample report. The spreadsheet instructions appear in Figure 6.10.

	A	B	C	D	E	F	G
1				MYCO INC.			
2			415 WEST	HARRISON	STREET		
3			JACKSON	CALIF.	94223		
4							
5			QUALITY	CONTROL	ANALYSIS		JAN. 1982
6	===
7	SAMPLE	WEIGHT	(X-XAV)	(X-XAV)^2			
8	1.00	**16.00**	0.01	.000064			
9	2.00	**16.02**	0.03	.000784			
10	3.00	**15.98**	-0.01	.000144			
11	4.00	**15.95**	-0.04	.001764			
12	5.00	**15.97**	-0.02	.000484			
13	6.00	**16.01**	0.02	.000324			
14	7.00	**15.99**	0.00	.000004			
15	8.00	**15.97**	-0.02	.000484			
16	9.00	**16.02**	0.03	.000784			
17	10.00	**16.00**	0.01	.000064			
18	11.00	**15.96**	-0.03	.001024			
19	12.00	**15.98**	-0.01	.000144			
20	13.00	**15.97**	-0.02	.000484			
21	14.00	**16.03**	0.04	.001444			
22	15.00	**16.02**	0.03	.000784			
23	16.00	**15.98**	-0.01	.000144			
24	17.00	**15.99**	0.00	.000004			
25	18.00	**15.96**	-0.03	.001024			
26	19.00	**16.03**	0.04	.001444			
27	20.00	**16.01**	0.02	.000324			
28							
29			SUM SQ	.01172			
30	N	20.00	MAX	16.03			
31	AVE	15.99	MIN	15.95			
32			STD DEV	.0242074			

Figure 6.9: QUALITY CONTROL ANALYSIS

```
/CY
/SL MASTER.VC
/GF$
C5:QUALITY        D5:CONTROL        E5:ANALYSIS        G5:JAN. 1982
A7:/FR
/R:B7.D7
A7:SAMPLE
  A8:1
  A9:+A8+1
  /R:A10.A27:R
B7:WEIGHT
```

Figure 6.10: Spreadsheet Instructions: QUALITY CONTROL ANALYSIS (continues)

```
       C7:"(X−XAV)
         C8:(B8−B31)
         /R:C9.C27:RN
       D7:"(X−XAV)^2
         D8:/FG +C8*C8
         /R:D9.D27:RR
       A30:N
         B30:@COUNT(B8.B27)
       A31:AVE
         B31:@AVE(B8.B27)
       C29:/FR
       /R:C30.C32
       C29:SUM SQ
         D29:@SUM(D8.D27)
       C30:MAX
         D30:@MAX(B8.B27)
       C31:MIN
         D31:@MIN(B8.B27)
       C32:STD DEV
         D32:/FG (D29/B30)^.5
```

Figure 6.10:

Spreadsheet Instructions: QUALITY CONTROL ANALYSIS (cont.)

We specify the sample numbers by writing:

A7:SAMPLE
A8:1
A9:+A8+1
/R:A10.A27:R

Next, we enter actual sample data into column B. To compute the number of samples and the average value, we write:

A30:N
B30:@COUNT(B8.B27)
A31:AVE
B31:@AVE(B8.B27)

We also calculate the difference, and the square of the difference between the sample value and the average:

B7:WEIGHT
C7:"(X−XAV)

```
        C8:(B8—B31)
        /R:C9.C27:RN
    D7:"(X—XAV)^2
        D8:/FG +C8*C8
        /R:D9.D27:RR
```

To obtain the sum of the squares, we write:

```
    C29:SUM SQ
        D29:@SUM(D8.D27)
```

Finally, we obtain the standard deviation and the minimum and maximum weights by writing:

```
    C30:MAX
        D30:@MAX(B8.B27)
    C31:MIN
        D31:@MIN(B8.B27)
    C32:STD DEV
        D32:/FG (D29/B30)^.5
```

HIRING PLAN

A major concern in any manufacturing company is to have the available personnel to meet production commitments. Efficient production dictates that there be an adequate staff—but that overstaffing not be allowed to occur. In this example we will use the VisiCalc program to combine production and sales forecasts to develop a hiring plan.

APPLICATION EXAMPLE

Let's assume that your manufacturing concern produces a wide variety of products. There are records available that show production times for the materials handling, machine shop, assembly, inspection and test departments. Using a sales forecast and the production times, you want to develop a spreadsheet that can generate hiring requirements.

SPREADSHEET INSTRUCTIONS

A printout of a hiring plan appears in Figure 6.11. The spreadsheet instructions are shown in Figure 6.12.

	A	B	C	D	E	F	G
1				MYCO INC.			
2			415 WEST HARRISON STREET				
3			JACKSON CALIF. 94223				
4							
5			HIRING PLAN			AUG. 1981	
6	==						
7		MANUF	TABLE	(HOURS)			
8	UNIT	MAT HAND	MACH SHP	ASSEM	INSPEC	TEST	
9	1	2	4	40	1	1	
10	2	3	0	50	1	2	
11	3	2	1	35	1	1	
12	4	4	5	80	2	1	
13							
14	ATTRITION	0.05					
15							
16							
17							
18			SALES	FORECAST (UNITS)			
19	UNIT	Q4(ACT)	Q1	Q2	Q3	Q4	
20	1	950	1000	1025	1050	1090	
21	2	780	800	830	865	890	
22	3	1525	1500	1450	1410	1370	
23	4	490	500	510	525	540	
24							
25							
26							
27							
28							
29	REQD						
30	MATL	9250	9400	9480	9615	9750	
31	MACH	7775	8000	8100	8235	8430	
32	ASSEM	169575	172500	174050	176600	179250	
33	INSPEC	4235	4300	4325	4375	4430	
34	TEST	4525	4600	4645	4715	4780	
35							
36	AVAIL						
37	MATL	19	19	19	19	20	
38	MACH	16	16	16	17	17	
39	ASSEM	343	349	352	357	363	
40	INSPEC	9	9	9	9	9	
41	TEST	9	9	9	10	10	
42							
43	HIRE						
44	MATL		1	1	1	1	
45	MACH		1	1	1	1	
46	ASSEM		23	21	23	23	
47	INSPEC		1	0	1	1	
48	TEST		1	1	1	1	

Figure 6.11: HIRING PLAN

```
    /CY
    /SL MASTER.VC
    /GOR
    /GFI
    C5:HIRING          D5:PLAN            G5:AUG. 1981
    B7:MANUF           C7:TABLE           D7:"(HOURS)
       A8:/FR
       /R:B8.F8
       A8:UNIT
          A9:1      A10:2      A11:3      A12:4
       B8:MAT HAND
       C8:MACH SHP
       D8:ASSEM
       E8:INSPEC
       F8:TEST
       A14:ATTRITION  B14:/F$
    C18:SALES          D18:FORECAST       E18:"(UNITS)
       A19:/FR
       /R:B19.F19
       A19:UNIT     B19:Q4(ACT)    C19:Q1     D19:Q2
       E19:Q3    F19:Q4
       A20:1     A21:2     A22:3     A23:4
       A29:REQD
          A30:MATL
          B30:(B20*B9)+(B21*B10)+(B22*B11)+(B23*B12)
          /R:C30.F30:RN RN RN RN
          A31:MACH
          B31:(B20*C9)+(B21*C10)+(B22*C11)+(B23*C12)
          /R:C31.F31:RN RN RN RN
          A32:ASSEM
          B32:(B20*D9)+(B21*D10)+(B22*D11)+(B23*D12)
          /R:C32.F32:RN RN RN RN
          A33:INSPEC
          B33:(B20*E9)+(B21*E10)+(B22*E11)+(B23*E12)
          /R:C33.F33:RN RN RN RN
```

Figure 6.12: Spreadsheet Instructions: HIRING PLAN (continues)

```
            A34:TEST
               B34:(B20*F9)+(B21*F10)+(B22*F11)+(B23*F12)
               /R:C34.F34:RN RN RN RN
         A36:" AVAIL
            A37:MATL
               B37:+B30/494
               /R:C37.F37:R
            A38:MACH
               B38:+B31/494
               /R:C38.F38:R
            A39:ASSEM
               B39:+B32/494
               /R:C39.F39:R
            A40:INSPEC
               B40:+B33/494
               /R:C40.F40:R
            A41:TEST
               B41:+B34/494
               /R:C41.F41:R
         A43:HIRE
            A44:MATL
               C44:/FI (C30—((1—B14)*B30))/494
               /R:D44.F44:RNR
            A45:MACH
               C45:/FI (C31—((1—B14)*B31))/494
               /R:D45.F45:RNR
            A46:ASSEM
               C46:/FI (C32—((1—B14)*B32))/494
               /R:D46.F46:RNR
            A47:INSPEC
               C47:/FI (C33—((1—B14)*B33))/494
               /R:D47.F47:RNR
            A48:TEST
               C48:/FI (C34—((1—B14)*B34))/494
               /R:D48.F48:RNR
```

Figure 6.12: Spreadsheet Instructions: HIRING PLAN (cont.)

We begin by creating a table that gives, for each unit produced, the number of hours required for each type of worker. (This table starts at coordinate B7.) We also give an average attrition rate in percentage form and a sales forecast by quarter.

Next, we calculate, for each type of worker, the total hours of labor. For example, we can obtain the machinists' hours by combining data from the sales forecast and the manufacturing statement. To do this, we write:

```
A31:MACH
  B31:(B20*C9)+(B21*C10)+(B22*C11)+(B23*C12)
  /R:C31.F31:RN RN RN RN
```

We calculate the number of workers needed per quarter by dividing the hours required by the number of hours per quarter:

```
A36:"#
  A38:MACH
    B38:+B31/494
    /R:C38.F38:R
```

We also assume for this example, that a worker is available 38 hours per week. Thus, to compute the number of workers we must hire, we subtract the present quarter hours from the next quarter hours, factor in attrition, and divide by the hours per quarter. For machinists, we write:

```
A43:HIRE
  A45:MACH
    C45:/FI (C31 — ((1 — B14)*B31))/494
    /R:D45.F45:RNR
```

SUMMARY

In this chapter, we have used the VisiCalc program to develop spreadsheets for various manufacturing situations. We have produced two simple, but very useful, spreadsheets for record-keeping applications, and we have developed several sophisticated mathematical forecasting examples.

7
REAL ESTATE

Mortgage Payment Schedule   Component Depreciation
Rental Versus Purchase Decision
Condominium Investment   Office Investment

OVERVIEW

In this chapter we will use the VisiCalc program to explore various real estate investment options. We will begin by creating a mortgage payment schedule. Given the amount of a loan, the terms, and the interest rate, this schedule can be used to compute the principal, interest, and remaining balance.

In the second example we will prepare a schedule that assigns different depreciation times to a building and to the depreciable items within.

Next, we will create a spreadsheet that can be used to determine if under certain circumstances it is more favorable to rent a home or to purchase one. Finally, we will use VisiCalc to analyze various real estate investments.

MORTGAGE PAYMENT SCHEDULE

In this first example we will use VisiCalc to set up a payment schedule for a property mortgage. Because we plan to examine various ranges of interest rates and repayment plans, we will place all the variables in a parameter table.

APPLICATION EXAMPLE

Let's assume that you have just obtained a loan and you need to prepare a schedule that determines the principal, interest payments, and remaining balance for the first three years of the loan. The payment required to fully amortize a loan is given by the following equation:

$$PMT = I*A/(1 - (V{\wedge}N))$$

where:

A = amount of original loan
I = interest rate per period (expressed as a decimal)
N = number of periods
V = $1/(1+I)$

The terms of the loan are:

A = 80,000
I = 16% annual interest
N = 30 years

SPREADSHEET INSTRUCTIONS

A sample printout of a payment schedule appears in Figure 7.1. Figure 7.2 shows the spreadsheet instructions. Let's examine them.

```
        A          B         C         D          E
1
2                            PAYMENT   SCHEDULE
3
4   LOAN AMOUNT          80000.00
5   INTEREST RATE           16.00
6   TERM                    30.00
7
8             I              .01
9             V              .99
10        PAYMENT         1075.81
11        V^N                .01
12        YEAR             1.00
13
14  MONTH  BALANCE  INTEREST  PRINCIP
15     1  79990.86
16     2  79981.60  1066.54      9.26
17     3  79972.22  1066.42      9.38
18     4  79962.71  1066.30      9.51
19     5  79953.07  1066.17      9.64
20     6  79943.31  1066.04      9.76
21     7  79933.41  1065.91      9.89
22     8  79923.38  1065.78     10.03
23     9  79913.22  1065.65     10.16
24    10  79902.93  1065.51     10.30
25    11  79892.49  1065.37     10.43
26    12  79881.92  1065.23     10.57
```

Figure 7.1: PAYMENT SCHEDULE

```
/CY
/GF$
/GOR
D2:PAYMENT        E2:SCHEDULE
A4:LOAN           B4:AMOUNT
A5:INTEREST       B5:RATE
A6:TERM
B8:" I
   C8:+C5/12/100
B9:" V
   C9:1/(1+C8)
B10:PAYMENT
   C10:+C4*C8/(1-(C9^(12*C6)))
B11:V^N
```

Figure 7.2: Spreadsheet Instructions: PAYMENT SCHEDULE (continues)

```
        C11:+C9^(12*C6)
   B12:YEAR
   A14:/FR
   /R:B14.D14
   A14:MONTH
        A15:/FI 1+(12*(C12−1))
        A16:/FI 1+A15
        /R:A17.A26:R
   B14:BALANCE
        B15:+C4/(C9^A15)*(C9^A15−C11)/(1−C11)
        /R:B16.B26:NNR NRN N
   C14:INTEREST
        C16:+C8*B15
        /R:C17.C26:NR
   D14:PRINCIP
        D16:+C10−C16
        /R:D17.D26:NR
```

Figure 7.2: Spreadsheet Instructions: PAYMENT SCHEDULE (cont.)

To begin, we place in a parameter table the figures for the original amount of the loan, the annual interest rate, and the length of time for which the loan was assumed.

We have designed this spreadsheet so that we make calculations in row rather than column order. To calculate I, V, and the payment, we write:

```
   B8:" I
      C8:+C5/12/100
   B9:" V
      C9:1/(1+C8)
   B10:PAYMENT
      C10:+C4*C8/(1−(C9^(12*C6)))
```

The formula that gives the balance remaining after any payment is:

$$\text{Bal(i)} = PV/(V^\wedge i * (V^\wedge i - (V^\wedge N))/(1 - (V^\wedge N))$$

where i is the number of the payment. Calculation can be speeded up by precomputing V^N. Thus, for this example we write:

```
B11:V^N
  C11:+C9^(12*C6)
```

We specify the year for which we display a payment schedule in coordinate C12. We calculate the number of the month from the beginning of the loan by writing:

```
A14:MONTH
  A15:/FI 1+(12*(C12−1))
  A16:/FI 1+A15
  /R:A17.A26:R
```

Next, we compute from the previously listed formula, the balance remaining after any payment:

```
B14:BALANCE
  B15:+C4/(C9^A15)*(C9^A15−C11)/(1−C11)
  /R:B16.B26:NNR NRN N
```

To compute the interest, we multiply the interest rate by the remaining balance. Thus, we write:

```
C14:INTEREST
  C16:+C8*B15
  /R:C17.C26:NR
```

Finally, to express the principal paid, we subtract the interest from the payment:

```
D14:PRINCIP
  D16:+C10−C16
  /R:D17.D26:NR
```

ADDITIONAL REMARKS

You can produce a payment schedule for any year in the term of a loan by simply specifying in cell C12 in the parameter table the year of the loan. You can also easily extend the number of years printed out; but, when doing this, take care not to create forward references.

COMPONENT DEPRECIATION

Real estate investors try to make use of income tax laws by attempting to convert ordinary income into capital gains, and thereby, reduce their income tax rate. This allows them to shelter their current income by writing-off cash expenses and depreciation.

Depreciation tax laws are in a constant state of flux. For example, during 1981 the depreciation time on real estate was reduced from 40 to 15 years. Depending on current tax laws, component depreciation may be another way to increase your tax write-offs. We will now develop a component depreciation schedule.

APPLICATION EXAMPLE

You wish to create a schedule that will allocate depreciation figures to a rental property on a component basis. You want to assign variable depreciation rates to the following items: the roof, carpets, drapes, kitchen appliances, furnace and water heater.

You want to first calculate depreciation on a straight-line basis for each component and then compute the total depreciation of the property.

SPREADSHEET INSTRUCTIONS

Figure 7.3 shows a completed component depreciation schedule. The spreadsheet instructions for this example appear in Figure 7.4.

We assign the values of the individual items and their life at data entry time. The entry labeled "BLDG" simply represents the entire building value, minus the value of the component parts. The formula for this calculation is:

```
A18:BLDG
   B18:+B5 − @SUM(B12.B17)
```

To obtain the individual depreciation amounts on a straight-line basis we divide the initial values by their useful lives:

```
D12:+B12/C12
/R:D13.D18:RR
```

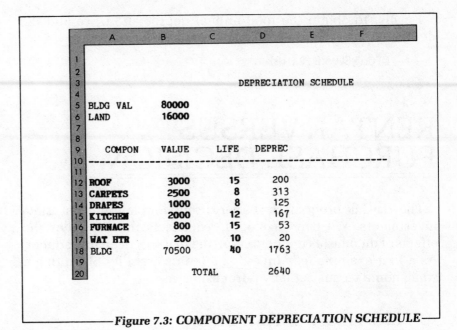

```
              A        B       C        D        E        F
 1
 2
 3                           DEPRECIATION SCHEDULE
 4
 5   BLDG VAL   80000
 6   LAND       16000
 7
 8
 9   COMPON     VALUE    LIFE    DEPREC
10   ------------------------------------------------------------
11
12   ROOF       3000      15      200
13   CARPETS    2500       8      313
14   DRAPES     1000       8      125
15   KITCHEN    2000      12      167
16   FURNACE     800      15       53
17   WAT HTR     200      10       20
18   BLDG      70500      40     1763
19
20                       TOTAL   2640
```

Figure 7.3: COMPONENT DEPRECIATION SCHEDULE

```
      /CY
      /GFI
      D3:DEPRECIAT      E3:ION SCHED     F3:ULE
      A5:BLDG VAL       A6:LAND
      A9:/FR
      /R:B9.F9
      A9:COMPON         B9:VALUE         C9:LIFE
      A10:/ — —
      /R:B10.E10
      A18:BLDG
         B18:+B5−@SUM(B12.B17)
      D9:DEPREC
         D12:+B12/C12
         /R:D13.D18:RR
      C20:TOTAL
         D20:@SUM(D12.D18)
```

Figure 7.4:
Spreadsheet Instructions: COMPONENT DEPRECIATION SCHEDULE

Finally, to obtain the total annual depreciation, we add the depreciation of the individual components:

D20:@SUM(D12.D18)

RENTAL VERSUS PURCHASE DECISION

The VisiCalc program can be very useful for planning real estate investments. We can develop spreadsheets that consider the effects of income tax deductions on the real cost of an investment. As a first example let's investigate the desirability of renting a small home versus actually purchasing one.

APPLICATION EXAMPLE

Let's assume that a couple is presently renting a home for $600 per month. They have the opportunity to purchase a home for $95,000, with 20% down and interest payments at 16% for 30 years. Their current income is $35,000, and their tax deductions are $5,000.

SPREADSHEET INSTRUCTIONS

Figure 7.5 shows a printout of a rental analysis spreadsheet. The spreadsheet instructions appear in Figure 7.6. Note that they include a parameter table. Let's examine them.

Since the loan balance equals the sale price, minus the down payment, we write:

B7:+B5−(B6/100*B5)

For this example, the interest rate, I, equals the annual interest stated in monthly terms. Thus, we write:

B11:+B8/12/100

Since V is defined as:

$$V = 1/(1+I)$$

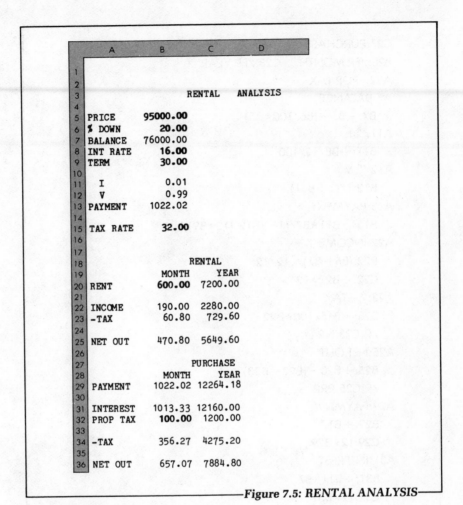

```
            A         B         C         D
 1
 2
 3                    RENTAL    ANALYSIS
 4
 5  PRICE    95000.00
 6  % DOWN      20.00
 7  BALANCE  76000.00
 8  INT RATE    16.00
 9  TERM        30.00
10
11    I          0.01
12    V          0.99
13  PAYMENT   1022.02
14
15  TAX RATE    32.00
16
17
18                     RENTAL
19             MONTH     YEAR
20  RENT      600.00   7200.00
21
22  INCOME    190.00   2280.00
23  -TAX       60.80    729.60
24
25  NET OUT   470.80   5649.60
26
27                    PURCHASE
28             MONTH     YEAR
29  PAYMENT  1022.02  12264.18
30
31  INTEREST 1013.33  12160.00
32  PROP TAX  100.00   1200.00
33
34  -TAX      356.27   4275.20
35
36  NET OUT   657.07   7884.80
```

Figure 7.5: RENTAL ANALYSIS

```
/CY
/GF$
C3:RENTAL          D3:ANALYSIS
A5:PRICE           A6:''% DOWN
A8:INT RATE        A9:TERM
A15:TAX RATE
C18:RENTAL         B19:/FR MONTH
C19:/FR YEAR       A20:RENT          C20:12*B20
```

Figure 7.6: Spreadsheet Instructions:
RENTAL VERSUS PURCHASE DECISION (continues)

```
C27:PURCHASE
B28:/FR MONTH    C28:/FR YEAR
A32:PROP TAX
A7:BALANCE
  B7:+B5−(B6/100∗B5)
A11:" I
  B11:+B8/12/100
A12:" V
  B12:1/(1+B11)
A13:PAYMENT
  B13:+B11∗B7/(1−(B12^(12∗B9)))
A22:INCOME
  B22:(B5−B7)∗.12/12
  C22:+B22∗12
A23:"−TAX
  B23:+B15/100∗B22
  /R:C23:NR
A25:NET OUT
  B25:+B20−(B22−B23)
  /R:C25:RRR
A29:PAYMENT
  B29:+B13
  C29:12∗B29
A31:INTEREST
  B31:+B11∗B7
  C31:12∗B31
  C32:12∗B32
A34:"−TAX
  B34:(B31+B32)∗B15/100
  C34:12∗B34
A36:NET OUT
  B36:+B29−B34−(B29−B31)
  /R:C36:RRRR
```

Figure 7.6: Spreadsheet Instructions:
RENTAL VERSUS PURCHASE DECISION (cont.)

in VisiCalc notation, we write:

B12:1/(1+B11)

We compute the payment as we discussed in the previous example:

B13:+B11*B7/(1−(B12^(12*B9)))

The rental portion of the spreadsheet shows the analysis for renting the home. We enter the monthly rent payment into B20. Since a down payment is necessary for buying a house, we make that amount available to earn interest. For this example 12% is assumed to be the annual market interest rate. Thus, we write:

B22:(B5−B7)*.12/12

However, we must reduce the income by the tax paid out. We do this by subtracting the after-tax income from the net cash outlay:

B23:+B15/100*B22
/R:C23:NR
B25:+B20−(B22−B23)
/R:C25:RRR

Let's now review the situation from the point of view of purchasing the home. The interest portion of the monthly payment is deductible. To obtain the interest paid for the first month, we multiply the monthly interest rate by the original balance; we then multiply this figure by twelve to approximate the actual interest payment. We could obtain an even more exact analysis by using the payment schedule expressed previously. Therefore, to obtain the interest we write:

B31:+B11*B7

We enter property tax as a data value. We obtain an income tax saving by reducing the taxable income. Next, we approximate the total effect of these tax savings by using the original tax rate. We write the tax saving as:

B34:(B31+B32)*B15/100

The net outlay is then:

Payment − Tax Saving − Equity

where:
$$\text{Equity} = \text{Payment} - \text{Interest}$$
Therefore, in VisiCalc notation, we write:
    B36: +B29−B34−(B29−B31)
We see that for this couple renting is a more economical alternative.

ADDITIONAL REMARKS

To see how rapidly the VisiCalc program can recalculate equations, try changing the income tax rate to 44% and printing a new report. The difference should be only $30 per month, as shown in Figure 7.7.

	A	B	C	D
1				
2				
3			RENTAL	ANALYSIS
4				
5	PRICE	95000.00		
6	% DOWN	20.00		
7	BALANCE	76000.00		
8	INT RATE	16.00		
9	TERM	30.00		
10				
11	I	0.01		
12	V	0.99		
13	PAYMENT	1022.02		
14				
15	TAX RATE	44.00		
16				
17				
18			RENTAL	
19		MONTH	YEAR	
20	RENT	600.00	7200.00	
21				
22	INCOME	190.00	2280.00	
23	−TAX	83.60	1003.20	
24				
25	NET OUT	493.60	5923.20	
26				
27			PURCHASE	
28		MONTH	YEAR	
29	PAYMENT	1022.02	12264.18	
30				
31	INTEREST	1013.33	12160.00	
32	PROP TAX	100.00	1200.00	
33				
34	−TAX	489.87	5878.40	
35				
36	NET OUT	523.47	6281.60	

Figure 7.7: Another Rental Analysis

Note: in both examples we have not accounted for any increase in the value of the home due to inflation. We will explore this factor in the next two examples.

CONDOMINIUM INVESTMENT

We will now expand the spreadsheet designed in the previous example to produce figures for a complete investment analysis. This type of analysis is done frequently to determine if purchasing real estate for rental purposes will prove to be a profitable investment.

APPLICATION EXAMPLE

Let's assume that you want to produce a general form that can be used to determine the profitability of investing in rental property. On this form you plan to include figures for a conventional first-mortgage payment, an interest-only second-mortgage payment, maintenance costs, vacancy factors, depreciation figures and other expenses. In addition, you plan to approximate the figures for equity buildup.

For this case let's assume that the value of the property being considered will inflate faster than the rental income and that you plan to sell the property in five years.

SPREADSHEET INSTRUCTIONS

A printout for this example appears in Figure 7.8. Figure 7.9 shows the spreadsheet instructions. Let's examine them.

It is important that we place all parameters in this example in a parameter table. That way, we can make assumptions and modify them easily. As shown in Figure 7.9 the parameter table occupies the beginning portion of the report. Note that all percentages are entered in the table in integer form. We later divide them by one hundred, prior to use, to put them in decimal form.

	A	B	C	D	E	F	G
1				MYCO INC.			
2			415 WEST	HARRISON	STREET		
3			JACKSON	CALIF.	94223		
4							
5			CONDO	INVESTMENT		MAR.	1982
6	==
7	SALES	PRICE	**125000**		MONTHLY	INCOME	650
8	DOWN	PAYMENT	**25000**		INF RATE	HOUSE	8
9	FIRST	AMOUNT	**75000**		INF RATE	RENT	3
10	FIRST	RATE	**13.75**		MAINT	RATE	1
11	FIRST	TERM	**25**		VACANCY	RATE	5
12	SECOND	BALANCE	25000		PROP TAX	RATE	1
13	SECOND	RATE	**14.00**		DEPREC	PERIOD	40
14					SALES	COMM	6
15		I=	0.14		TAX RATE		50
16		V=	0.88		OTHER	EXP RATE	1
17							
18							
19							
20							
21							
22	--
23		1982	1983	1984	1985	1986	
24	PROP VAL	125000	135000	145800	157464	170061	
25							
26	INCOME	7410	7632	7861	8097	8340	
27	FIRST	10741	10741	10741	10741	10741	
28	SECOND	3500	3500	3500	3500	3500	
29	MAINT	1250	1350	1458	1575	1701	
30	PROP TAX	1250	1350	1458	1575	1701	
31	OTHER	1250	1350	1458	1575	1701	
32							
33	CASH FLOW	-10581	-10659	-10754	-10868	-11003	
34							
35	LOAN BAL	74571	74083	73529	72897	72179	
36	EQ PAID	429	488	555	631	718	
37	DEPR	3125	3125	3125	3125	3125	
38	TAX INC	-13278	-13296	-13324	-13362	-13410	
39	TAX	-6639	-6648	-6662	-6681	-6705	
40							
41	NET CASH	-3943	-4011	-4092	-4187	-4298	
42							
43	SALES PRI	183666					
44	COMM	11020					
45	GAIN	63271					
46	TAX	12654					
47							
48	FIRST	72179					
49	SECOND	25000					
50	NET	62812					

Figure 7.8: CONDOMINIUM INVESTMENT

```
/CY
/SL MASTER.VC
/GOR
/GFI
D5:CONDO        E5:INVESTMEN    F5:T            G5:MAR. 1982
A7:SALES        B7:PRICE
A8:DOWN         B8:PAYMENT
A9:FIRST        B9:AMOUNT
A10:FIRST       B10:RATE        C10:/F$
A11:FIRST       B11:TERM
A12:SECOND      B12:BALANCE
A13:SECOND      B13:RATE        C13:/F$
E7:MONTHLY      F7:INCOME
E8:INF RATE     F8:HOUSE
E9:INF RATE     F9:RENT
E10:MAINT       F10:RATE
E11:VACANCY     F11:RATE
E12:PROP TAX    F12:RATE
E13:DEPREC      F13:PERIOD
E14:SALES       F14:COMM
E15:TAX         F15:RATE
E16:OTHER       F16:EXP RATE
A22:/ — —
/R:B22.G22
A23:/FI
/R:B23.F23
B23:1982        C23:1983        D23:1984
E23:1985        F23:1986
   C12: + C7 — C8 — C9
   B15:I=
      C15:/F$ + C10/100
   B16:V=
      C16:/F$ 1/(1 + C15)
   A24:PROP VAL
      B24: + C7
```

Figure 7.9: Spreadsheet Instructions: CONDOMINIUM INVESTMENT (continues)

```
        C24: +B24*(1+(G8/100))
        /R:D24.F24:RN
    A27:FIRST
        B27: +C9*C15/(1−(C16^C11))
        /R:C27.F27:NNNN
    A28:SECOND
        B28: +C12*C13/100
        /R:C28.F28:NN
    A26:INCOME
        B26:12*G7*(1−(G11/100))
        C26: +B26*(1+(G9/100))
        /R:D26.F26:RN
    A29:MAINT
        B29: +B24*G10/100
        /R:C29.F29:RN
    A30:PROP TAX
        B30: +B24*G12/100
        /R:C30.F30:RN
    A31:OTHER
        B31: +B24*G16/100
        /R:C31.F31:RN
    A33:CASH FLOW
        B33: +B26 − @SUM(B27.B31)
        /R:C33.F33:RRR
    A35:LOAN BAL
        B35: +C9−(B27−(C15*C9))
        C35: +B35−(B27−(C15*B35))
        /R:D35.F35:RRNR
    A36:EQ PAID
        B36: +C9−B35
        C36: +B35−C35
        /R:D36.F36:RR
    A37:DEPREC
        B37: +C7/G13
        /R:C37.F37:NN
```

Figure 7.9:
Spreadsheet Instructions: CONDOMINIUM INVESTMENT (continues)

```
        A38:TAX INC
            B38: +B33+B36−B37
            /R:C38.F38:RRR
        A39:TAX
            B39: +G15/100*B38
            /R:C39.F39:NR
        A41:NET CASH
            B41: +B33−B39
            /R:C41.F41:RR
        A43:SALES PRICE
            B43: +F24*(1+(G8/100))
        A44:COMM
            B44: +B43*G14/100
        A45:GAIN
            B45: +B43−B44−C7+@SUM(B37.F37)
        A48:FIRST
            B48: +F35
        A49:SECOND
            B49: +C12
        A46:TAX
            B46: .4*G15/100*B45
        A50:NET
            B50: +B43−B44−B46−B48−B49
```

Figure 7.9:
Spreadsheet Instructions: CONDOMINIUM INVESTMENT (cont.)

Maintenance costs, property taxes, and other expenses are based on the current value of the property. Therefore, we must be sure that the current value is readily available. For this reason we make it the first quantity that we calculate and print. Using the standard compounding technique, we write:

```
B24: +C7
C24: +B24*(1+(G8/100))
/R:D24.F24:RN
```

We calculate I, V, and the first mortgage using the same formulas that we used in the previous example. Here, however, we compute these figures on an annual rather than monthly basis. We then use the annual results to estimate equity buildup. Therefore, we write:

```
B15:I=
    C15:/F$ +C10/100
B16:V=
    C16:/F$ 1/(1+C15)
A27:FIRST
    B27:+C9*C15/(1-(C16^C11))
    /R:C27.F27:NNNN
A28:SECOND
    B28:+C12*C13/100
    /R:C28.F28:NN
```

Next, we compute the cash flows and enter these figures in the income statement. We multiply the rental income by twelve-times the monthly income; we then multiply this result by the vacancy factor. Finally, we compound the result at the rental inflation rate:

```
A26:INCOME
    B26:12*G7*(1-(G11/100))
    C26:+B26*(1+(G9/100))
    /R:D26.F26:RN
```

Maintenance costs, property taxes and other expenses are based on the current property value. Thus, we write:

```
A29:MAINT
    B29:+B24*G10/100
    /R:C29.F29:RN
A30:PROP TAX
    B30:+B24*G12/100
    /R:C30.F30:RN
A31:OTHER
    B31:+B24*G16/100
    /R:C31.F31:RN
```

We compute the cash flow by subtracting the expenses from the income:

```
A33:CASH FLOW
    B33:-SUM(B27.B31)+B26@
    /R:C33.F33:RRR
```

The loan balance equals the balance at the beginning of the year, minus the difference of the payments and the interest paid:

A35:LOAN BAL
    B35: +C9 − (B27 − (C15∗C9))
    C35: +B35 − (B27 − (C15∗B35))
    /R:D35.F35:RRNR

The annual equity paid is the difference between the loan balance figures at the beginning and the end of the year:

A36:EQ PAID
    B36: +C9 − B35
    C36: +B35 − C35
    /R:D36.F36:RR

The taxable income is then the cash flow, plus the equity, minus the depreciation. To calculate depreciation and taxable income, we write:

A37:DEPREC
    B37: +C7/G13
    /R:C37.F37:NN
A38:TAX INC
    B38: +B33 + B36 − B37
    /R:C38.F38:RRR

We then use the tax rate to compute the income tax by writing:

A39:TAX
    B39: +G15/100∗B38
    /R:C39.F39:NR

Since the net cash flow equals the before-tax cash flow, minus the income tax, we write:

A41:NET CASH
    B41: +B33 − B39
    /R:C41.F41:RR

The property is to be sold at the end of five years. We calculate the sales price by inflating the 1986 property value. We then calculate the real estate commission from the sales price and commission rate. We express the sales price and commission as:

```
A43:SALES PRICE
    B43: +F24*(1+(G8/100))
A44:COMM
    B44: +B43*G14/100
```

To compute the capital gain, we subtract the purchase price from the net sales price and add back the depreciation:

```
A45:GAIN
    B45: +B43-B44-C7+@SUM(B37.F37)
```

The tax rate for capital gains is 40% of the ordinary rate. To compute the tax, we write:

```
A46:TAX
    B46: .4*G15/100*B45
```

Finally, the net cash received is equal to the net sales price, minus the tax and mortgages due:

```
A50:NET
    B50: +B43-B44-B46-B48-B49
```

OFFICE INVESTMENT

We will now use the real estate investment model that we developed in the previous example to analyze many different types of real estate projects.

APPLICATION EXAMPLE

Let's assume that you are the new owner of an office building. You plan to rent out most of the office space in the building and need to determine the best rental rates. To do this you plan to analyze various rate projections and determine how they will affect your cash flow. You plan to make your projections by the quarter.

SPREADSHEET INSTRUCTIONS

The printout for this example appears in Figure 7.10. The spreadsheet instructions are given in Figure 7.11. We have set up the spreadsheet to reflect a quarterly projection. Therefore, we will convert all figures that have been previously stated in monthly terms to reflect the projection by quarters. We have set up the spreadsheet so that when we give the figures for the number of units rented per quarter, *all* the cash flows will be computed.

```
                        MYCO INC.
                415 WEST HARRISON STREET
                JACKSON  CALIF.  94223

                   OFFICE    INVESTMENT
=================================================================
SALES   PRICE      300000       MONTHLY  INCOME          650
DOWN    PAYMENT     40000       INF RATE HOUSE             8
FIRST   AMOUNT     240000       INF RATE RENT             3
FIRST   RATE        13.75       MAINT    RATE             1
FIRST   TERM           25       VACANCY  RATE             5
SECOND  BALANCE     20000       PROP TAX RATE             1
SECOND  RATE        14.00       DEPREC   PERIOD          40
                                SALES    COMM             6
          I=         0.14       TAX RATE                 50
          V=         0.88       OTHER    EXP RATE         1


        ----------------------------------------------------------
                    Q1        Q2        Q3        Q4
UNITS               0         1         1         3

INCOME              0      1950      1950      5850

FIRST            8530      8530      8530      8530
SECOND            700       700       700       700
EXPENSES         5250      5250      5250      5250

CASH FLOW      -14480    -12530    -12530     -8630

DEPR             1875      1875      1875      1875

TAX INC        -16355    -14405    -14405    -10505

TAX             -8177     -7202     -7202     -5252

NET CASH        -8177     -7202     -7202     -5252
```

Figure 7.10: OFFICE INVESTMENT

Note: We will begin by loading the CONDOMINIUM INVEST-
MENT spreadsheet and deleting rows 23 through 50. We will
then input the following spreadsheet instructions:

```
        D5:OFFICE
        B23:/FR
        /R:C23.F23
        B23:Q1              C23:Q2          D23:Q3          E23:Q4
        A24:UNITS
        A26:INCOME
            B26:3*G7*B24
            /R:C26.E26:NR
        A28:FIRST
            B28:+C9/4*C15/(1-(C16^C11))
            /R:C28.E28:NNNN
        A29:SECOND
            B29:+C13*C12/100/4
            /R:C29.E29:NN
        A30:EXPENSES
            B30:@SUM(G10.G12)*C7*3/12/100
            /R:C30.E30:NNN
        A32:CASH FLOW
            B32:+B26-@SUM(B28.B30)
            /R:C32.E32:RRR
        A34:DEPR
            B34:+C7/G13/4
            /R:C34.E34:NN
        A36:TAX INC
            B36:+B32-B34
            /R:C36.E36:RR
        A38:TAX
            B38:+G15/100*B36
            /R:C38.E38:NR
        A40:NET CASH
            B40:+B36-B38
            /R:C40.E40:RR
```

Figure 7.11: Spreadsheet Instructions: OFFICE INVESTMENT

We begin by entering the figures for the number of units in positions B24 through E24. We write the income as:

```
A26:INCOME
    B26:3*G7*B24
    /R:C26.E26:NR
```

where G7 contains the monthly rent and B24 contains the projected number of rented units. Next, we write the expressions for the first and second mortgages:

```
A28:FIRST
    B28:+C9/4*C15/(1−(C16^C11))
    /R:C28.E28:NNNN
A29:SECOND
    B29:+C13*C12/100/4
    /R:C29.E29:NN
```

To calculate expenses we add the various percentages and multiply by the original property value. We express this as:

```
A30:EXPENSES
    B30:@SUM(G10.G12)*C7*3/12/100
    /R:C30.E30:NNN
```

We then calculate the cash flow:

```
A32:CASH FLOW
    B32:+B26−@SUM(B28.B30)
    /R:C32.E32:RRR
```

As in the previous example the projection will be complete when we include the depreciation and the effect of taxes.

SUMMARY

In this chapter we have prepared spreadsheets for use in real estate investment analyses. As we have stressed throughout this book, once you understand the principles used to develop these examples, you can easily develop additional models.

INCOME TAXES

Preliminary Information
Schedule B   Schedule E   Form 1040, Page 1
Schedule A   Form 1040, Page 2   Schedule Y

OVERVIEW

In this chapter we will use the VisiCalc program to develop spreadsheets that are useful for planning and preparing federal income tax reports. We will design these spreadsheets so that they are similar in appearance to actual federal forms.

The VisiCalc program is an ideal tool for preparing income tax reports as it offers many useful features for analyzing various tax situations. For example, if it is necessary to change an income or deduction figure, the VisiCalc program will immediately recalculate a new tax total.

This chapter shows you how to design tax forms and implement tax tables. You should be able to use these design methods to build new spreadsheets as the federal forms undergo their inevitable, annual changes.

PRELIMINARY INFORMATION

APPLICATION EXAMPLE

You plan to use the VisiCalc program to prepare your federal income tax reports. You will begin by preparing a spreadsheet on which you will record the necessary preliminary data.

SPREADSHEET INSTRUCTIONS

Figure 8.1 displays the preliminary spreadsheet. Figure 8.2 shows the spreadsheet instructions used to prepare it. Let's examine them.

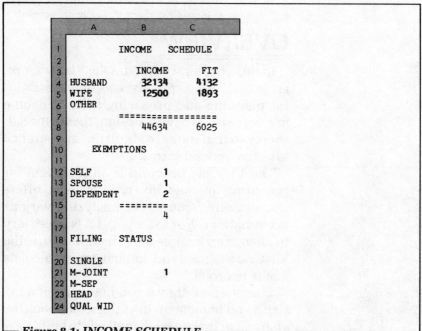

```
            A        B        C
 1              INCOME   SCHEDULE
 2
 3                INCOME      FIT
 4  HUSBAND       32134     4132
 5  WIFE          12500     1893
 6  OTHER
 7              ==================
 8                44634     6025
 9
10     EXEMPTIONS
11
12  SELF              1
13  SPOUSE            1
14  DEPENDENT         2
15              =========
16                    4
17
18  FILING   STATUS
19
20  SINGLE
21  M-JOINT          1
22  M-SEP
23  HEAD
24  QUAL WID
```

Figure 8.1: INCOME SCHEDULE

```
/CY
B1:INCOME        C1:SCHEDULE
    A4:HUSBAND       A5:WIFE           A6:OTHER
    B3:/FR INCOME
       B8:@SUM(B4.B6)
    C3:/FR FIT
       C8:@SUM(C4.C6)
    B7:/-=           C7:/-=
A10:/FR EXEMP    B10:TIONS
    A12:SELF         A13:SPOUSE        A14:DEPENDENT
       B15:/-=
```

Figure 8.2: Spreadsheet Instructions: INCOME SCHEDULE (continues)

```
        B16:@SUM(B12.B14)
A18:FILING          B18:STATUS
  A20:SINGLE
  A21:M—JOINT
  A22:M—SEP
  A23:HEAD
  A24:QUAL WID
```

Figure 8.2: Spreadsheet Instructions: INCOME SCHEDULE (cont.)

We begin by entering at coordinates B4 and B5, the incomes for the husband and wife. We record the tax withheld at positions C4 and C5. We enter any additional income at C6. We then add these figures, using VisiCalc formulas:

B8:@SUM(B4.B6)

C8:@SUM(C4.C6)

Next, we enter onto the spreadsheet all information concerning exemptions and filing status. To declare exemptions, we enter a 1 by the category "self," and, if appropriate, a 1 for a spouse. We enter the number of dependent exemptions at position B14. Finally, we enter a single 1 in the appropriate filing status box.

SCHEDULE B

The first federal form that we will complete is Schedule B. This form is used to record interest and dividend income. We will add it to the previous spreadsheet.

APPLICATION EXAMPLE

You want to design a spreadsheet that displays your tax information for Schedule B.

SPREADSHEET INSTRUCTIONS

Figure 8.3 shows a completed Schedule B spreadsheet. The instructions for this spreadsheet appear in Figure 8.4. In this

```
      E      F       G       H    I    J     K      L      M
 1
 2
 3                              SCHEDULE B
 4
 5
 6
 7  INTEREST INCOME                      DIVIDEND INCOME
 8
 9
10
11
12
13                              NAME OF PAYER
14                              AT&T                   >      200
15            PAYER             PG&E                   >      300
16  1A INTEREST INC             SAFEWAY  STORES        >      200
17                                                     >
18  WORLD SAVINGS      >     546                       >
19  BANK OF AMERICA    >     782                       >
20  DREYFUS FUND       >    2345                       >
21                     >                               >
22                     >                               >
23                     >                               >
24                     >                               >
25                     >                               >
26                     >                               >
27                     >                               >
28                     >                               >
29                     >                               >
30                     >                               >
31                     >                               >
32                     >                               >
33                     >                               >
34                     >                               >
35  1B TOTAL                3673                       >
36  1C ASC INTEREST                                    >
37                                                     >
38                                                     >
39
40  B OF A         >   1200        4 TOTAL                    700
41                 >              5 CAP GAIN
42                 >              DIST            >
43                 >
44                 >              6 NONTAX
45  1D TOTAL          1200        DIST            >
46  1E EXC            2000        7 TOTAL   5+6                 0
47                                8 TOTAL   4-7               700
48  1F                             0
49
50
51
52  2 TOTAL                3673
```

Figure 8.3: *SCHEDULE B*

chapter we will precede user-entered data with the ">" symbol. Thus, column G has a series of ">" symbols. These symbols indicate that the interest amounts are to be entered in column H.

```
H3:/FR              SCHED          I3:ULE B
E7:INTEREST         F7:INCOME
  E15:/FR PAY    F15:ER
  E16:"1A INTERE F16:ST INC
    G18:/FR    ">
    /R:G19.G34
  E35:"1B TOTAL
    H35:@SUM(H18.H34)
  E36:"1C ASC IN    F36:TEREST
    F40:/FR     ">
    /R:F41.F44
  E45:"1D TOTAL
      G45:@SUM(G40.G44)
  E46:"1E EXC
      G46:@IF(B16=1,1000,2000)
  E48:"1F
    H48:@IF(F45>F46,+F45-F46,0)
  E52:"2 TOTAL
    H52:+H35+H48
I7:DIVIDEND         J7:INCOME
  I13:NAME OF P     J13:AYER
    K14:/FR    ">
    /R:K15.K39
  I40:"4 TOTAL
    L40:@SUM(L14.L39)
  I41:"5 CAP GAI   J41:N      I42:DIST        J42:/FR   ">
  I44:"6 NON TAX   I45:DIST   J45:/FR   ">
  I46:"7 TOTAL     J46:"5+6
    L46:+J42+J45
  I47:"8 TOTAL     J47:"4-7
    L47:+L40-L46
```

Figure 8.4: Spreadsheet Instructions: SCHEDULE B

With one exception the only VisiCalc formula that we use on this spreadsheet is the @SUM function. We use it to specify column totals. For example:

```
E35:"1B TOTAL
    H35:@SUM(H18.H34)
```

For All-Savers Certificates (ASC), an interest exclusion of $1,000 is allowed for a single taxpayer and $2,000 for married taxpayers. We use the exemption information from the preliminary spreadsheet to calculate the ASC exclusions:

```
E46:"1E EXC
    G46:@IF(B16=1,1000,2000)
E48:"1F
    H48:@IF(F45>F46,+F45−F46,0)
```

The first expression tests whether the exclusion is $1,000 or $2,000; the second tests whether or not the ASC interest exceeds the exclusion. Any excess is treated as income.

SCHEDULE E

There are several schedules that handle income received. As an example of how you can turn these schedules into VisiCalc spreadsheets, we will now specify side 1 of Schedule E in spreadsheet format. Again, we add this to the previous spreadsheet.

SPREADSHEET INSTRUCTIONS

Figure 8.5 shows a Schedule E printed in spreadsheet format. The spreadsheet instructions for this display appear in Figure 8.6. Specification of the spreadsheet is quite straightforward; let's examine some of the details.

Schedule E is set up to keep track of three different properties. On line 19 we add the sum of the depreciation expenses from line 18 and the itemized expenses from line 17. Thus, we write:

```
E113:"19 TOTAL
    H113:+H108+H110
    /R:I113.J113:RR
```

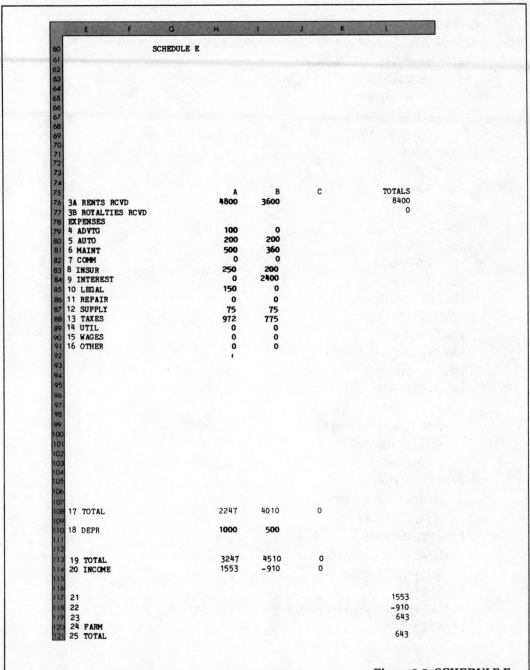

	A	B	C		TOTALS
3A RENTS RCVD	4800	3600			8400
3B ROYALTIES RCVD					0
EXPENSES					
4 ADVTG	100	0			
5 AUTO	200	200			
6 MAINT	500	360			
7 COMM	0	0			
8 INSUR	250	200			
9 INTEREST	0	2400			
10 LEGAL	150	0			
11 REPAIR	0	0			
12 SUPPLY	75	75			
13 TAXES	972	775			
14 UTIL	0	0			
15 WAGES	0	0			
16 OTHER	0	0			
17 TOTAL	2247	4010	0		
18 DEPR	1000	500			
19 TOTAL	3247	4510	0		
20 INCOME	1553	-910	0		
21					1553
22					-910
23					643
24 FARM					
25 TOTAL					643

SCHEDULE E

Figure 8.5: SCHEDULE E

```
   G60:SCHEDULE       H60:E
H75:/FR A              I75:/FR B              J75:/FR C
   E76:"3A RENTS       F76:RCVD
   E77:"3B ROYALT      F77:IES RCVD
      L75:/FR TOTALS
         L76:@SUM(H76.J76)
         L77:@SUM(H77.J77)
E78:EXPENSES
   E79:"4 ADVTG
   E80:"5 AUTO
   E81:"6 MAINT
   E82:"7 COMM
   E83:"8 INSUR
   E84:"9 INTEREST
   E85:"10 LEGAL
   E86:"11 REPAIR
   E87:"12 SUPPLY
   E88:"13 TAXES
   E89:"14 UTIL
   E90:"15 WAGES
   E91:"16 OTHER
   E108:"17 TOTAL
      H108:@SUM(H79.H91)
      /R:I108.J108:RR
   E110:"18 DEPR
   E113:"19 TOTAL
      H113:+H108+H110
      /R:I113.J113:RR
   E114:"20 INCOME
      H114:+H76+H77−H113
      /R:I114.J114:RRR
   E117:"21
      L117:@IF(H114>0,H114,0)+@IF(J114>0,J114,0)+@IF(I114>0,I114,0)
   E118:"22
```

Figure 8.6: Spreadsheet Instructions: SCHEDULE E (continues)

```
    L118:@IF(H114<0,H114,0)+@IF(J114<0,J114,0)+@IF(I114<0,I114,0)
E119:"23
    L119:+L117+L118
E120:"24 FARM
E121:"25 TOTAL
    L121:+L119+L120
```

Figure 8.6: Spreadsheet Instructions: SCHEDULE E (cont.)

Next, we obtain the total income by subtracting the expenses from the gross receipts:

```
E114:"20 INCOME
    H114:+H76+H77−H113
    /R:I114.J114:RRR
```

On line 21 we sum the properties with profits, and on line 22 we sum the properties with losses. We use the @IF function to test whether the profit is positive or negative. On line 20 the output of the @IF test is either a positive profit or a zero. We reverse this test on line 21 to add negative profits. We express these tests as:

```
E117:"21
    L117:@IF(H114>0,H114,0)+@IF(J114>0,J114,0)+@IF(I114>0,I114,0)
E118:"22
    L118:@IF(H114<0,H114,0)+@IF(J114<0,J114,0)+@IF(I114<0,I114,0)
```

Finally, we obtain the total profit by combining the amounts from lines 21 and 22:

```
E119:"23
    L119:+L117+L118
```

ADDITIONAL REMARKS

You can create spreadsheets for other income related forms, such as Schedules C and D, by simply specifying these forms in a manner similar to the previous example.

FORM 1040, PAGE 1

We will now combine the income spreadsheets with manually entered income figures to specify page 1 of the 1040 form.

SPREADSHEET INSTRUCTIONS

A sample 1040 spreadsheet appears in Figure 8.7. Figure 8.8 presents the spreadsheet instructions.

We previously entered the figure for total wages on the income spreadsheet. We will now post this to the 1040 spreadsheet by writing:

        M30:"7 WAGES E   N30:TC
        T30: +B8

Likewise we also post the interest and dividend income from the Schedule A spreadsheet:

        M31:"8A INTERE   N31:ST
        R31: +H52
        M32:"8B DIVIDE   N32:NDS
        R32: +L47

Next, we add the numbers in coordinates 8A and 8B, and then subtract the dividend exclusion. Married persons filing joint returns are entitled to a $400 exclusion; others are entitled to $200. We test the exemptions with the @IF function on the income spreadsheet to generate the exclusion. We also use the @IF test with the subtraction so that a negative amount is not generated. Thus we write:

        M33:"8C TOTAL
        R33: +R31 +R32
        M34:"8D EXCLUS   N34:ION
        R34:@IF(B21 =1,400,200)
        M35:"8E C —D
        T35:@IF((R33 —R34)>0,R33 —R34,0)

On the income tax spreadsheets we frequently use the test shown

```
        M    N    O    P    Q    R    S    T
 1              FORM 1040 PAGE 1
 2
 3
 4
 5
 6
 7
 8
 9
10
11
12
13
14
15
16
17
18
19
20
21
22
23
24
25
26
27
28
29
30   7 WAGES ETC                                        44634
31   8A INTEREST                          3673
32   8B DIVIDENDS                          700
33   8C TOTAL                             4373
34   8D EXCLUSION                          400
35   8E C-D                                             3973
36   9 REFUND OF STATE                         >         442
37     INCOME TAX
38  10 ALIMONY RECVD                            >          0
39  11 BUSINESS INC (C)                         >          0
40  12 CAP GAIN (D)                             >          0
41  13 40% OF CAP GAIN DIST                     >          0
42  14 SUPP GAINS (4797)                        >          0
43  15 TAXABL PENSIONS                          >          0
44  16A OTHER PENSIONS                 >                   0
45  16B TAX AMOUNT P10                          >          0
46  17 RENTS (E)                                         643
47  18 FARM INCOME (F)                          >          0
48  19A UNEMP INS                      >                   0
49  19B TAX AMOUNT P10                          >          0
50  20 OTHER                                    >          0
51
52  21 TOTAL                                             49692
53  22 MOVING EXPENSE                     >        0
54  23 EMPLOYEE BUSINESS EXP             >     1500
55  24 IRA                                >       .0
56  25 KEOGH                              >      112
57  26 INTEREST PENALTY                   >        0
58  27 ALIMONY PAID                       >        0
59  28 DIS INC EXCLUS                     >        0
60  29 OTHER
61  30 TOTAL                                             1612
62  31 ADJ GROSS INC                                     48080
```

Figure 8.7: FORM 1040, PAGE 1

```
P1:FORM 1040      Q1:/FR PAGE 1
M30:"7 WAGES E    N30:TC
   T30:+B8
M31:"8A INTERE    N31:ST
   R31:+H52
M32:"8B DIVIDE    N32:NDS
   R32:+L47
M33:"8C TOTAL
   R33:+R31+R32
M34:"8D EXCLUS    N34:ION
   R34:@IF(B21=1,400,200)
M35:"8E C−D
   T35:@IF((R33−R34)>0,R33−R34,0)
M36:"9 REFUND     N36:OF STATE                           S36:/FR  ">
M37:" INCOME      N37:TAX
M38:"10 ALIMON    N38:Y RCVD                             S38:/FR  ">
                                                         /R:S39.S40

M39:"11 BUSINE    N39:SS INC (C      O39:")
M40:"12 CAP GA    N40:IN (D)

M41:"13 40% OF    N41:" CAP GAIN   O41:" DIST    S41:/FR  ">
                                                         /R:S42.S43

M42:"14 SUPP G    N42:AINS (479     O42:"7)
M43:"15 TAXABL    N43:" PENSIONS
M44:"16A OTHER    N44:" PENSIONS                         Q44:/FR  ">
M45:"16B TAX A    N45:MOUNT P10                          S45:/FR  ">
M46:"17 RENTS     N46:"(E)
   T46:+L121
M47:"18 FARM I    N47:NCOME (F)                          S47:/FR  ">
M48:"19A UNEMP    N48:" INS                              Q48:/FR  ">
M49:"19B TAX A    N49:MOUNT P10                          S49:/FR  ">
M50:"20 OTHER                                            S50:/FR  ">
M52:"21 TOTAL
```

Figure 8.8: Spreadsheet Instructions: FORM 1040, PAGE 1 (continues)

```
    T52:@SUM(T30.T50)
    M53:"22 MOVING  N53:" EXPENSE                Q53:/FR  ">
                                                 /R:Q54.Q59

    M54:"23 EMPLOY   N54:EE BUSINE   O54:SS EXP
    M55:"24 IRA
    M56:"25 KEOGH
    M57:"26 INTERE   N57:ST PENALT                O57:Y
    M58:"27 ALIMON   N58:Y PAID
    M59:"28 DIS IN   N59:C EXCLUS
    M60:"29 OTHER
    M61:"30 TOTAL
      T61:@SUM(R53.R60)
    M62:"31 ADJ GR   N62:OSS INC
      T62:+T52—T61
```

Figure 8.8: Spreadsheet Instructions: FORM 1040, PAGE 1 (cont.)

at coordinate T35. This test is set up so that the difference between two quantities results in zero if the difference is negative; otherwise, the actual subtraction occurs.

The rest of the spreadsheet is easily specified; we won't review it here.

SCHEDULE A

Let's now turn our attention to Schedule A, the form used to itemize deductions. We will review here the spreadsheet instructions that require Boolean functions.

SPREADSHEET INSTRUCTIONS

Figure 8.9 shows a completed Schedule A spreadsheet, and Figure 8.10 shows the spreadsheet instructions. Let's examine these instructions.

```
        AA      AB      AC      AD      AE      AF      AG      AH
 1                          SCHEDULE A
 2
 3
 4
 5
 6
 7
 8
 9  MEDICAL                         CONTIBUTIONS
10                                   21 CASH              >        800
11  1 1/2 BUT LESS THAN    >     150                      >
12    150 OF INSUR                                        >
13                                                        >
14  2 DRUGS        >       77                             >
15  3 1% OF  1040       480.80                            >
16    LINE 31                                             >
17  4 2-3                  60.88                          >
18  5 BAL OF INS      >   200                             >
19                                                        >
20  6 OTHER                          22 OTHER            >
21  A DRS ETC         >  2400                            >
22  B HOSP            >   275  23 CARRYOVER              >
23  C TRANS           >   375  24 TOTAL                          800
24  D OTHER           >     0       CASUALTY
25                     >
26                     >
27                     >
28                     >          25 LOSS               >        300
29                     >
30                     >          26 REIMB              >        150
31                     >                                >
32  7 TOTAL           3250.00 27 25-26                          150
33  8 3% 1040 LINE 31 1442.40 28 100 OR LINE 27
34  9 7-8             1807.60    SMALLEST                       100
35
36  10 TOTAL         1957.60 29 TOTAL                           50
37                              MISC
38  TAXES                      30A UNION DUES           >         0
39  11 STATE & LOC INC  >   843 30B TAX PREPARE         >       100
40  12 REAL  ESTATE     >  1200 31 OTHER                >
41  13 GENERAL SALES    >   440                         >
42     MOTOR VEH SALES  >     0                         >
43  14 PERS  PROP       >     0                         >
44  15 OTHER            >     0                         >
45                      >                               >
46                      >                               >
47                      >          32 TOTAL                      100
48  16 TOTAL              2483 SUMMARY
49
50  INTEREST                    33 MED                        1957.60
51  17 MORT             >  5553 34 TAXES                        2483
52  18 CREDIT CARD      >   321 35 INT                          5874
53  19 OTHER            >     0 36 CONTR                         800
54                      >          37 LOSS                        50
55                      >          38 MISC                       100
56                      >          39 TOTAL                   11264.60
57                      >          40 EXEMP                     3400
58                      >
59                      >
60                      >          41 39-40                    7864.60
61  20 TOTAL             5874
```

Figure 8.9: SCHEDULE A

```
AD1:SCHEDULE      AE1:A
AA9:MEDICAL
    AA11:"1 1/2 BUT    AB11:" LESS THA    AC11:N                  >
    AA12" 150 OF       AB12:INSUR
    AA14:"2 DRUGS      AB14:/FR ">
    AA15:"3 1% OF      AB15:"1040
    AA16:" LINE 31
        AC15:.01*T62
    AA17:"4 2-3
        AD17:@IF((AC14-AC15)>0,AC14-AC15,0)
    AA18:"5 BAL OF    AB18:INS        AC18:/FR   ">
    AA20:"6 OTHER
        AA21:A DRS ETC                AC21:/FR   ">
                                      /R:AC22.AC31

        AA22:B HOSP
        AA23:C TRANS
        AA24:D OTHER
    AA32:"7 TOTAL
        AD32:@SUM(AD17.AD24)
    AA33:"8 3% 1040   AB33:/FR LINE 31
        AD33:.03*T62
    AA34:"9  7-8
        AD34:@IF((AD32-AD33)>0,AD32-AD33,0)
    AA36:"10 TOTAL
        AD36:+AD34+AD11
AA38:TAXES
    AA39:"11 STATE     AB39:"& LOC INC  AC39:/FR   ">
                                        /R:AC40.AC47

    AA40:"12 REAL      AB40:ESTATE
    AA41:"13 GENERA AB41:L SALES
    AA42:"  MOTOR      AB42:VEH SALES
    AA43:"14 PERS      AB43:PROP
    AA44:"15 OTHER
    AA48:"16 TOTAL
        AD48:@SUM(AD39.AD47)
```

Figure 8:10: Spreadsheet Instructions: SCHEDULE A (continues)

```
AA50:INTEREST
   AA51:"17 MORT                    AC51:/FR  ">
                                    /R:AC52.AC60

     AA52:"18 CREDIT   AB52:CARD
          AA53:"19 OTHER
          AA61:"20 TOTAL
          AD61:@SUM(AD51.AD60)
     AE9:CONTRIBUTI         AF9:ONS
          AE10:" 21 CASH              AG10:/FR  ">
                                      /R:AG11.AG22

          AE20:" 22 OTHER
          AE22:" 23 CARRY       AF22:OVER
          AE23:" 24 TOTAL
            AH24:@SUM(AH10.AH22)
     AE25:CASUALTY
          AE28:" 25 LOSS               AG28:/FR  ">
                                       /R:AG29.AG31

          AE30:" 26 REIMB
          AE32:" 27 25-26
            AH32:@IF((AH28-AH30)>0,AH28-AH30,0)
          AE33:" 28 100 O     AF33:R LINE 27
          AE34:/FR SMALL      AF34:EST
            AH34:@IF(AH32<100,AH32,100)
          AE36:" 29 TOTAL
            AH36:+AH32-AH34
     AE37:MISC
          AE38:" 30A UNIO   AF38:N DUES     AG38:/FR  ">
                                           /R:AG39.AG46

          AE39:" 30B TAX    AF39:PREPARE
          AE40:" 31 OTHER
          AE47:" 32 TOTAL
            AH47:@SUM(AH38.AH46)
     AE48: SUMMARY
          AE50:" 33 MED
            AH50:+AD36
```

Figure 8.10: Spreadsheet Instructions: SCHEDULE A (continues)

```
    AE51:" 34 TAXES
        AH51: +AD48
    AE52:" 35 INT
        AH52: +AD61
    AE53:" 36 CONTR
        AH53: +AH23
    AE54:" 37 LOSS
        AH54: +AH36
    AE55:" 38 MISC
        AH55: +AH47
    AE56:" 39 TOTAL
        AH56: @SUM(AH50.AH55)
    AE57:" 40 EXEMP
        AH57: @IF(B20=1,2300,0)+ @IF(B21=1,3400,0)
            + @IF(B22=1,1700,0)+ @IF(B23=1,3400,0)
    AE60:" 41 39−40
        AH60: @IF(AH56−AH57>0,AH56−AH57,@FALSE)
```

Figure 8.10: Spreadsheet Instructions: SCHEDULE A (cont.)

On line 3 of Schedule A we enter 1% of the income from line 31 of form 1040. Next, we subtract line 3 from line 2 and, provided a positive result occurs, we enter the result on line 4. We use the @IF function to accomplish this test. Thus, we write:

```
    AC15:.01*T62
    AA17:"4 2−3
    AD17: @IF((AC14−AC15)>0,AC14−AC15,0)
```

Similarly, line 8 requires that 3% of line 31 be subtracted from line 7. Thus, we write:

```
    AD33:.03*T62
    AA34:"9 7−8
    AD34: @IF((AD32−AD33)>0,AD32−AD33,0)
```

The calculation of casualty loss includes a $100 exclusion and a test to insure that a negative amount is not generated. As above, we specify this as:

```
    AE32:" 27 25−26
    AH32: @IF((AH28−AH30)>0,AH28−AH30,0)
    AH34: @IF(AH32<100,AH32,100)
```

At line 40 of Schedule A we enter the dollar amounts of the exemptions that result from the filing status indicated on the income spreadsheet. We state these in tabular form as:

FILING STATUS	AMOUNT
1 or 4	2300
2 or 5	3400
3	1700

Next, we use the @IF function to determine the exemption amount from the filing status boxes on the income spreadsheet. Since only one box is checked, only one of the four tests listed below will yield a non-zero result. Thus, the exemption amount becomes:

```
AE57:" 40 EXEMP
   AH57:@IF(B20=1,2300,0)+@IF(B21=1,3400,0)
      +@IF(B22=1,1700,0)+@IF(B23=1,3400,0)
```

Line 41 requires that line 40 be subtracted from line 39. In the event that the amount in line 40 is greater than the amount in line 39, the user is to refer to the 1040 instructions on page 20. We indicate this by printing a FALSE. Thus, we write this subtraction as:

```
AE60:" 41 39−40
   AH60:@IF(AH56−AH57>0,AH56−AH57,@FALSE)
```

FORM 1040, PAGE 2

We are now ready to complete the second side of the 1040 Form. (*Warning:* At this point it is important to check the memory indicator on your CRT. If you have less than 12K available, you will need to start a new spreadsheet file.)

SPREADSHEET INSTRUCTIONS

A completed spreadsheet is shown in Figure 8.11. The spreadsheet instructions are shown in Figure 8.12.

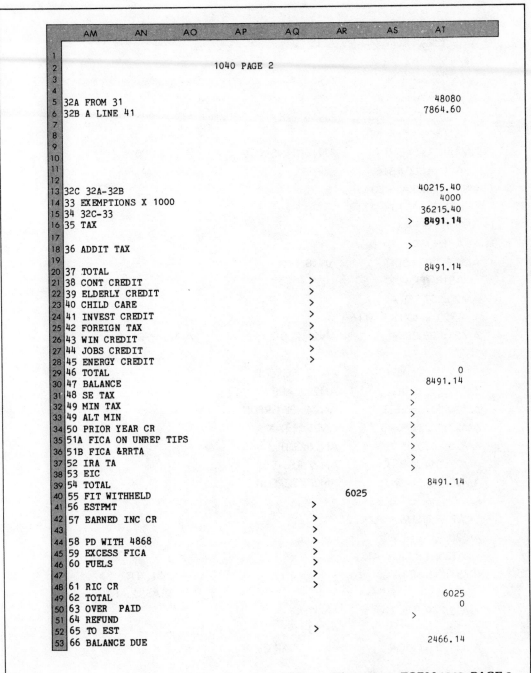

Figure 8.11: FORM 1040, PAGE 2

```
AP2:"1040 PAGE      AQ2:" 2
AM5:"32A FROM       AN5:"31
   AT5:+T62
AM6:"32B A LIN      AN6:E 41
   AT6:+AH60
AM13:"32C 32A-3     AN13:"2B
   AT13:+AT5-AT6
AM14:"33 EXEMPT     AN14:IONS X 10      AO14:"00
   AT14:1000*B16
AM15:"34 32C-33
   AT15:+AT13-AT14
AM16:"35 TAX
   AS16:/FR   ">
AM18:"36 ADDIT      AN18:TAX
   AS18:/FR   ">
AM20:"37 TOTAL
   AT20:+AT18+AT16
AM21:"38 CONT C     AN21:REDIT          AQ21:/FR   ">
                                        /R:AQ22.AQ28

AM22:"39 ELDERL     AN22:Y CREDIT
AM23:"40 CHILD      AN23:CARE
AM24:"41 INVEST     AN24:/FR CREDIT
AM25:"42 FOREIG     AN25:N TAX
AM26:"43 WIN CR     AN26:EDIT
AM27:"44 JOBS C     AN27:REDIT
AM28:"45 ENERGY     AN28:" CREDIT
AM29:"46 TOTAL
   AT29:@SUM(AR21.AR28)
AM30:"47 BALANC     AN30:E
   AT30:+AT20-AT29
AM31:"48 SE TAX                         AS31:/FR   ">
                                        /R:AS32.AS38

AM32:"49 MIN TA     AN32:X
AM33:"49 ALT MI     AN33:N
AM34:"50 PRIOR      AN34:YEAR CR
```

Figure 8.12: Spreadsheet Instructions: FORM 1040, PAGE 2 (continues)

```
AM35:"51A FICA        AN35:ON UNREP        AO35:TIPS
AM36:"51B FICA        AN36:"&RRTA
AM37:"52 IRA TA       AN37:X
AM38:"53 EIC
AM39:"54 TOTAL
  AT39:@SUM(AT30.AT38)
AM40:"55 FIT WI       AN40:THHELD
  AR40:+C8
AM41:"56 ESTPMT                            AQ41:/FR   ">
                                           /R:AQ42.AQ48

AM42:"57 EARNED       AN42:" INC CR
AM44:"58 PD WIT       AN44:H 4868
AM45:"59 EXCESS       AN45:" FICA
AM46:"60 FUELS
AM48:"61 RIC CR
AM49:"62 TOTAL
  AT49:@SUM(AR40.AR48)
AM50:"63 OVER         AN50:PAID
  AT50:@IF(AT49>AT39,AT49−AT39,0)
AM51:"64 REFUND
  AS51:/FR   ">
AM52:"65 TO EST
  AQ52:/FR   ">
AM53:"66 BALANC       AN53:E DUE
  AT53:@IF(AT39>AT49,AT39−AT49,0)
```

Figure 8.12: Spreadsheet Instructions: FORM 1040, PAGE 2 (con't)

We begin by transferring the figure for the gross income from line 31, and the figure for the deductions from line 41:

```
AM5:"32A FROM        AN5:"31
  AT5:+T62
AM6:"32B A LIN        AN6:E 41
  AT6:+AH60
```

Next, we subtract lines 32A and 32B and put the result on line 32C. We then obtain the taxable income by multiplying the number of exemptions by $1,000 and subtracting the results from line 32C.

Thus, we write:

> AM13:"32C 32A−3   AN13:"2B
>   AT13: +AT5−AT6
> AM14:"33 EXEMPT   AN14:IONS X 10   AO14:"00
>   AT14:1000∗B16
> AM15:"34 32C−33
>   AT15: +AT13−AT14

Note: If it was necessary for you to previously divide your spreadsheet into two files because of memory limitation, you must enter the following lines manually:

> 32A
> 32B
> 33
> 55

Line 35 is where we enter the actual tax amount. Depending on the user's situation, this tax is obtained from either a tax table or one of three tax rate schedules, Schedule D, G, or Form 4726. We have designed the spreadsheet so that we enter the tax manually from the appropriate schedule or table. In the next section we show how to implement one of these schedules.

Lines 36 through 62 involve simple data entries and column summations. Let's now examine lines 63 through 66.

Line 63 is to be entered as overpaid if line 62 exceeds line 54. We calculate this with the @IF function by writing:

> AM50:"63 OVER   AN50:PAID
>   AT50:@IF(AT49>AT39,AT49−AT39,0)

Lines 64 and 65 are to be entered manually by the user. Line 66 is entered if line 54 exceeds line 62. Again we use the @IF function:

> AM53:"66 BALANC   AN53:E DUE
>   AT53:@IF(AT39>AT49,AT39−AT49,0)

This completes our analysis of the spreadsheet instructions.

SCHEDULE Y

This section designs a VisiCalc spreadsheet that will automate the calculation of income tax for Schedule Y. Similar methods may be used to automate other tax schedules.

SPREADSHEET INSTRUCTIONS

Figure 8.13 shows a completed spreadsheet for Schedule Y. The spreadsheet instructions appear in Figure 8.14.

	BA	BB	BC	BD	BE	BF
1						
2						
3			SCHED Y			
4	34760.48					
5						
6	0	0	0	0	0	0
7	3400	0	3400	.14	3400	3400
8	5500	294	5500	.16	5500	5500
9	7600	630	7600	.18	7600	7600
10	11900	1404	11900	.21	11900	11900
11	16000	2265	16000	.24	16000	16000
12	20200	3273	20200	.28	20200	20200
13	24600	4505	24600	.32	24600	24600
14	29900	6201	29900	.37	29900	29900
15	35200	8162	35200	.43	35200	35200
16	45800	12720	45800	.49	45800	45800
17	60000	19678	60000	.54	60000	60000
18	85600	33502	85600	.59	85600	85600
19	109400	47544	109400	.64	109400	109400
20	162400	81464	162400	.68	162400	162400
21	215400	117504	215400	.7	215400	215400
22						
23	TAX					
24	BASE		6201			
25	EXCESS		4860.48			
26	EX TAX		1798.38			
27						
28	TAX		7899.384			

Figure 8.13: SCHEDULE Y

AC24:TAX INC
   BA4:+AT15
BC2:SCHED Y

BA6:0	BB6:0	BD6:0
BA7:3400	BB7:0	BD7: .14
BA8:5500	BB8:294	BD8: .16
BA9:7600	BB9:630	BD9: .18
BA10:11900	BB10:1404	BD10: .21
BA11:16000	BB11:2265	BD11: .24
BA12:20200	BB12:3273	BD12: .28
BA13:24600	BB13:4505	BD13: .32

Figure 8.14: Spreadsheet Instructions: SCHEDULE Y (continues)

```
     BA14:29900        BB14:6201         BD14: .37
     BA15:35200        BB15:8162         BD15: .43
     BA16:45800        BB16:12720        BD16: .49
     BA17:60000        BB17:19678        BD17: .54
     BA18:85600        BB18:33502        BD18: .59
     BA19:109400       BB19:47544        BD19: .64
     BA20:162400       BB20:81464        BD20: .68
     BA21:215400       BB21:117504       BD21: .70
  BA6:/R.BA21:BC6
  BA6:/R.BA21:BE6
  BA6:/R.BA21:BF6
  BB23:TAX
  BB24:BASE
     BC24:@LOOKUP(BA4,BA6.BA21)
  BB25:EXCESS
     BC25:+BA4−@LOOKUP(BA4,BE6.BE21)
  BB26:EX TAX
     BC26:/F$ +BC25*@LOOKUP(BA4,BC6.BC21)
  BB28:TAX
     BC28:/F$ +BC24+BC26−(.0125*(BC24+BC26))
```

Figure 8.14: Spreadsheet Instructions: SCHEDULE Y (cont.)

Tax is determined from Schedule Y as follows:

1. Using the amount of taxable income from line 34 of Form 1040, we look at the schedule and find the lower end of the tax range, and the table tax amount for this number.

2. Next, we subtract the lower range number from the taxable income, and multiply the difference by the percentage amount shown in the table.

3. Next, we add the base tax. We then add on the percentage tax to obtain the total tax.

4. Finally, we reduce the tax by .0125 of the amount of the tax.

We can easily accomplish all of these steps using the VisiCalc program. We must first, however, create three lookup tables. The first table consists of the two locations, BA6 and BB6; we used it to determine the base tax. The second table, in locations BC6 and BD6, provides the percentage tax factor. The final table gives the lower end of the base amount. To use these tables to compute the tax, we implement the LOOKUP function to determine the base tax by writing:

BB24:BASE

    BC24:@LOOKUP(BA4,BA6.BA21)

We then use the LOOKUP function again to find the excess over the base amount:

BB25:EXCESS

    BC25: +BA4− @LOOKUP(BA4,BE6.BE21)

Finally, we find the total tax by "looking up" the excess percentage factor, multiplying this percentage by the excess, and then adding the amounts just computed and applying the percentage reduction factor. We write this as:

BB26:EX TAX

    BC26:/F$ +BC25＊@LOOKUP(BA4,BC6.BC21)

BB28:TAX

    BC28:/F$ +BC24+BC26−(.0125＊(BC24+BC26))

SUMMARY

In this chapter, we have used the VisiCalc program to implement several federal income tax forms as spreadsheets. We have also learned to implement one of the tax rate schedules. Note that the techniques presented in this chapter can also be used to prepare spreadsheets for other tax forms.

CONCLUSION

As we have shown in this book, the VisiCalc program has numerous applications. The examples we have presented have ranged from very simple business ledgers to more complex forecasting models. Each example has been designed so that it can either be used directly or easily adopted to a particular situation by simply implementing a few changes. You should now be familiar enough with the VisiCalc program to design and prepare your own spreadsheets for your own applications. The author hopes that when you do, you will have as much fun as he had preparing the examples for this book, and that you will let him know of any unusual applications you may develop.

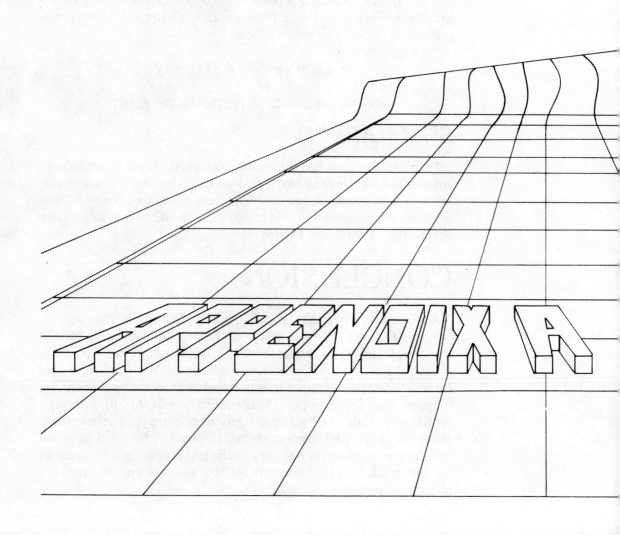

APPENDIX A: VISICALC CONVENTION AND COMMAND SUMMARY

THE VISICALC CONVENTIONS

LABELS

Labels are any combination of letters or symbols used to identify items in a row or column. A label must begin with either a letter or quote sign ("). You enter a label by moving the cursor to the desired coordinate and typing in the label.

Legal label entries

June

Rate %

Jan. 1, 1981

" 1984

Illegal label entries

3 June

.sum

(YTD)

dozen

In general, you can make an illegal label legal by simply placing a quotation sign before the label entry. For example:

(YTD)   (illegal)

"(YTD)   (legal)

VALUES

Values are numbers—either entered or computed. A value can contain a decimal point, a positive or a negative sign, or it can be entered in scientific notation. A value cannot contain a comma.

> *Legal value entries*
>
> 123
> −123.2
> 1.23E2   *(scientific notation)*
>
> *Illegal value entries*
>
> $123
> 123,456

EXPRESSIONS

An *expression* (or formula) can consist of values (numbers), co-ordinates of other values or expressions, functions, operators, or parentheses. An expression must start with either a digit, a plus or minus sign, a decimal, a parenthesis, or, if it is the start of a function, an @ sign.

If you use a coordinate of another value in an expression, the VisiCalc program will use the value in the referenced coordinate when evaluating the expression.

> *Legal expressions*
>
> 4+3
> 5*(3+2)
> 3*@PI
> 6+B4   *(adds 6 to value in B4)*
>
> *Illegal expressions*
>
> B4+6   *(needs to start with +)*
> 3+A   *(A is not a coordinate)*

OPERATORS

Legal operators in VisiCalc are +, −, *, /, and ^. These symbols represent:

+	Addition
−	Subtraction
*	Multiplication
/	Division
^	Exponentiation

The exponentiation operator raises a value to the power indicated.

Examples:

$4^2 = 16$ *(4 squared)*
$4^{(1/2)} = 2$ *(square root of 4)*

Logical Operators

Logical operators compare two values. The logical value TRUE is returned if the comparison is as stated; otherwise, FALSE is returned.

Operator	Operation
<	Less Than
>	Greater Than
=	Equal To
<=	Less Than or Equal To
>=	Greater Than or Equal To
<>	Not Equal To

Order of Expression Evaluation

Expressions are evaluated on a strict left to right basis. There is one exception, however; quantities within parentheses are always evaluated first. Care must be used when writing expressions; otherwise, incorrect results may occur.

Examples:

$$4+2 = 6$$
$$2+4 = 6$$
$$2+4*2 = 12$$
$$2+(4*2) = 10$$
$$9^{(1/2)} = 3$$
$$9^1/2 = 4.5$$

BUILT-IN FUNCTIONS

VisiCalc contains many *built-in functions* to simplify the writing of frequently encountered expressions. These functions always begin with an @ sign followed by the function itself and an expression in parentheses (called an *argument*). If the argument is a value, V, it may be any legal VisiCalc value. That is, V can be a constant or a coordinate position.

Some functions refer to the argument as a list. A *list* may be a combination of values, expressions, and ranges, separated by commas.

A *range* refers to a sequence of column or row positions that begin and end with the stated coordinates. The coordinates are separated by a period.

Examples:

E6.F6
A7.D7

A summary of the VisiCalc functions follows.

THE VISICALC FUNCTIONS SUMMARY

@ABS(V)—returns the absolute value of V.

Examples:

@ABS(3) = 3
@ABS(−3) = 3
B5: (−5)
@ABS(B5) = 5

@AVE(list)—calculates the average value of the entries in a list. Blank entries in a list are ignored.

Examples:

@AVE(1,2,3) = 2
@AVE(B1.B3) average of values in B1, B2, B3

@CHOOSE(v,list)—chooses one of a list of values. The number, v, is the position in the list that is selected.

Examples:

@CHOOSE(3,10,20,30,40) = 30
@CHOOSE(2,B1.B4) = value of B2

@COUNT(list)—results in the number of non-zero entries in a list.

@EXP(V)—gives the result of raising the constant e (2.71823) to the v power. This expression is entirely equivalent to (2.71823)^(V).

@LN(V)—computes the natural logarithm of a number, V.

@LOG10(V)—computes the logarithm to the base 10 of a number.

@LOOKUP(V,RANGE)—looks up values in a table and finds the first value that is larger than the one being looked up. The function then yields the table value just prior to the one that was found. For columns, the lookup tables are in the column to the right of the range. For rows, the tables are just below the range.

@MAX(list)—provides the maximum value in a list.

@MIN(list)— provides the minimum value in a list.

@NPV(i,range)—calculates the net present value of a series of cash flows. The cash flows are to be in the range. The discount rate used is the value i. Cash flows must be in the order to be received and are at the end of the period.

@SQRT(V)—provides the square root of a value and is equivalent to V^(1/2).

@SUM(list)—adds all numbers in a list.

Example:
B1:2 B2:4 B3:6
@SUM(12,B1.B3,10)=34

TRIGONOMETRIC FUNCTIONS

VisiCalc can compute the trigonometric functions in radians. Legal trigonometric functions are:

@SIN(V)
@COS(V)
@TAN(V)
@ASIN(V)
@ACOS(V)
@ATAN(V)

The last three functions are arc functions.

THE VISICALC COMMANDS

THE BLANK COMMAND
SYNTAX: /B

The BLANK command erases the label, value, or expression at the current cursor location. It does not affect format specification.

THE CLEAR COMMAND
SYNTAX: /C

The CLEAR command erases all information on the current spreadsheet. Before clearing, however, the prompt line asks you to type Y to confirm. CLEAR has the following effects. It:

1. erases all the information
2. places the cursor at A1
3. causes the direction indicator to indicate horizontal (on Apple II computers)
4. resets formats, titles, and windows to the values that they held when the spreadsheet was loaded.

THE DELETE COMMAND
SYNTAX: /D(R,C)

The DELETE command automatically removes an entire row or column from the VisiCalc spreadsheet. Prior to typing the command, you must place the cursor in the row or column you want to delete. After you type the prompt line D reads:

DELETE:RC

R deletes the row the cursor is in and C deletes the column. The VisiCalc program then fills in the deleted row or column as follows:

- The rows below the deleted row all move up one row. The columns to the right of the deleted column move left one column.

- Expressions containing coordinate references are adjusted according to the moves that are made.

Example:

A1:+C1+2

If column B is deleted, column C will shift left to become the new column B and then the expression is:

A1:+B1+2

THE EDIT COMMAND

SYNTAX: /E(ESC,←,→,char)

The EDIT command allows you to make corrections on a label, a value, or an expression, without having to retype it. To use the EDIT command you place the cursor over the coordinate that is to be modified, and then type /E. The edit cursor is moved left or right with either the left or right arrow key. Typing any character will then insert that character to the left of the edit cursor. Typing ESC will remove the character to the left of the edit cursor.

Example:

A1:4+3*2

To add parentheses to the above expression, type /E. By pressing the right arrow key two times you can place the edit cursor over the 3. Now by simply typing a left parentheses you can add it to the formula. Now press the right arrow four times and type a right parenthesis. The edit line should read:

A:4+(3*2)

THE FORMAT COMMAND

SYNTAX: /F(D,G,I,R,$,*)

The FORMAT command is used to modify the information displayed on the VisiCalc screen or on a hard copy report. The actual stored data is unaffected by this command.

The FORMAT command will modify the format of any coordinate on which the cursor is positioned. You can re-format an entire row by formatting the first position, and then replicating the format across the row. *Caution:* you must do this prior to data entry or the data in the first position will be replicated over the entire row. However, an individual position may be formatted without affecting the stored contents.

Let's examine some of the individual format options.

Default (/FD)   resets the entry position format to the Global format currently in use. If you have not previously set the Global format, the format will be set to the General format.

General (/FG)   displays all values in decimal or scientific notation, depending on the number of significant digits. Labels are left adjusted; values are right adjusted. A leading blank is added to values.

Integer (/FI)   displays all values in integer form, rounded to the nearest whole number.

Left Justification (/FL)   left-justifies numbers, with one leading blank. Integer format will no longer be in effect in that entry position.

Right Justification (/FR)   moves a label to the right, provided the label has fewer characters than the column width.

Dollar Format (/F$)   displays all values in dollars and cents format (two decimal places).

Bar Graph Format (/F*)   rounds the local value to the nearest integer and displays the same number of asterisks that is equal to the local integer value.

THE GLOBAL COMMAND

SYNTAX: /G(C(#), O(R,C), R(A,M), F(D,G,I,L,R,$,*))

The GLOBAL command has four options that cause universal action on the entire VisiCalc sheet. If more than one window is in effect, the global refers to the window on which the cursor resides.

Global Column (/GC#)   changes the width of all columns to the number (#) entered. Column width may be between 3 and 37. There is no provision for adjustment of individual column widths.

Global Order (/GO(R,C))   determines the order of recalculation for an entire VisiCalc sheet. When the VisiCalc program is first loaded, recalculation order is by columns. That is, first the expression in A1 is evaluated, then A2, etc. After the end of column A, expression evaluation goes to B1. You can change the recalculation order to rows by typing:

/GOR

and then back to columns again by typing:

/GOC

Recalculation by rows means the order will be A1B1 . . . A1B2, etc.
    To obtain reliable results, an expression must be evaluated before it is referenced by another expression. If it is not, an error condition, called a *forward reference,* will occur. You should carefully plan your VisiCalc forms, and carefully choose your order of recalculation, so that foward references do not occur.

Global Recalculation (/GR(A,M))   each time a value or expression is changed, the VisiCalc program recalculates the entire spreadsheet. This can cause undesirable delays. These delays may be overcome by typing:

/GRM

Recalculation will then cease until you type:

/GRA

and the automatic mode is resumed. You may also recalculate by typing an exclamation mark.

Global Format (/GF(D,G,I,L,R,$,*)) works like the format command we just described, except that it applies to the entire VisiCalc spreadsheet, rather than an individual entry position.

THE GO TO COMMAND

> SYNTAX: > COORD

The GO TO command moves the cursor from its current location to the coordinate specified after the (>).

THE INSERT COMMAND

> SYNTAX: /I(R,C)

The INSERT command inserts a blank row or column into the current VisiCalc spreadsheet. If the INSERT ROW command is used, a row is inserted into the position where the cursor currently resides. The current row and all subsequent rows are then shifted down by one row. If the INSERT COLUMN option is used, a column is inserted at the current cursor location. The current row and all subsequent rows are then shifted right by one column.

When the INSERT command is used, expressions containing coordinates are adjusted so that they reflect the new coordinates.

> *Examples:*

> A1: +C1+2

If the cursor is now placed over column B and a column is inserted, the new formula for A1 becomes:

> A1: +D1+2

Let's now make some additional observations. Many built-in functions include a range of values; for example:

> @ SUM (B1 . . . H1)

If a column is inserted between B1 and H1, the new sum will be correct and it will be:

> @ SUM (B1 . . . I1)

The column, however, may not be inserted at row B. Also, a column or row may not be inserted in the row or column that contains the sum.

THE MOVE COMMAND

SYNTAX: /M . . . COORD

The MOVE command moves an entire column or row. Expressions are then recalculated to reflect the new coordinates. To move a row down, place the cursor on the desired row, and type /M. Next, type in the coordinate (in the same column) of the row below the destination row.

To move a row up, place the cursor on the desired row, and type /M. Now type in the coordinate (in the same column) of the destination row.

To move a column right, place the cursor on the desired column, and type /M. Type in the coordinate of the column one column to the right of the desired column.

To move a column left, place the cursor on the desired column. Type in the coordinate of the desired column.

THE PRINT COMMAND

SYNTAX: /P(P,F)

There are some differences in the use of this command between various computers and printers. Consult your VisiCalc manual for specifics. A general discussion of the PRINT options follows.

PRINT Options

To print your VisiCalc spreadsheets, first, define the portion of the spreadsheet to be printed by placing the cursor at the upper left coordinate of the portion of the report to be printed, then type /P. A prompt line will appear asking for the setup string and the lower right coordinate. Consult your VisiCalc manual for the correct response to the setup string. (Often you must type a string or minus sign in order to obtain the correct number of linefeeds with your computer and printer.) Finally, type in the lower right coordinate that is to be printed.

Print Format File

This option of the PRINT command works in exactly the same way as the option described previously, except that the output becomes a diskette file, and is, therefore, not transferred to the printer. This allows the file to be read by a BASIC or word processor program.

To exercise this command, you place the cursor at the upper left coordinate of the material you wish to transfer to disk and type

/PF (file name)

After typing the file name, respond to the prompt line by typing the lower right coordinate. The PRINT file will be saved on diskette as a standard system file. It may be edited with a text editor, or read with a BASIC program, a Pascal program, or a word processor.

THE PRINT FORMULAS COMMAND

SYNTAX: /SS,S

The PRINT FORMULAS command prints all formulas and formats for the VisiCalc spreadsheet. Formulas are printed from the lower right to the upper left coordinate.

THE REPEAT LABEL COMMMAND

SYNTAX: /—

This VisiCalc command fills the cursor coordinate position with the sequence of characters indicated after the hyphen. Most often the command is used to draw a line of dashes, equal signs, or asterisks.

As an example, you can draw a line of asterisks across an entire spreadsheet by using the REPEATING LABEL command in combination with the REPLICATE command. This can be done as follows:

A3: /—*
/R:B3.H3

THE REPLICATE COMMAND

SYNTAX: /R

The REPLICATE command copies labels, values, and expressions from one coordinate to another. The REPLICATE command can also copy all of the expressions and labels in one row to another row.

Copying Labels and Values   To copy labels and values, place the cursor on the coordinate to be copied and invoke the REPLICATE command by typing /R. The program will prompt with

REPLICATE: SOURCE RANGE OR RETURN

If only a single position is to be copied, you simply press the return key. If a row or column is to be copied, you must type a period followed by the ending coordinate. The prompt line now becomes:

REPLICATE: TARGET RANGE

You now enter either a single coordinate or a range of co-ordinates.

Examples:

    A1:
    /R:C1:   (*Copy a single entry to a single position.*)
    /R:C1.E1:   (*Copy a single entry to multiple positions.*)
    /R.A3:C1.E1: (*Copy a column into three rows.*)

Copying Expressions   To copy expressions, you follow the steps discussed above, but, in addition, you must indicate either *relative* or *no change* for each coordinate position in the expression. You type N for no change and R for relative.

As an example, let's assume a constant is located in coordinate C1 and you wish B1 to equal A1 multiplied by C1; B2 to equal A2 multiplied by C1, etc. The sequence below accomplishes this multiplication.

Example:

    B1:+C1*A1
    /R:B2.B10:NR

(*Note:* In this book, for reasons of legibility, we have put spaces between the groups of N's and R's whenever long replicate sequences occur. These spaces do not need to be keyed in.)

Example:

    /R:B3.B10:RRR NRR RRN

THE STORAGE COMMAND

SYNTAX: /S (L,S,D,I,Q,#)

The STORAGE command loads and saves forms on diskette. The forms stored on diskettes are called files and are referred to by their file names. It is recommended that a file name consist of a recognizable name, followed by a period and an extension. Common extensions are VC for forms, DIF for DIF files, and PF for PRINT FORMAT files. File names can be up to eight characters long and must start with a letter.

Examples:

> FORECAST.VC   *(a report form)*
> SALES.DIF   *(daily sales in DIF)*
> INVENT.PF   *(inventory in print format)*

Loading From Diskette (/SL)   To load a previously stored file from diskette, simply type /SL and the file name, where the file name is the complete name of the previously saved file.

The LOAD command does not clear any previous forms from memory. If you are loading an individual form, first clear the memory by using the CLEAR command. Although it is possible to combine information from two forms without using the CLEAR command, the two reports must not use overlapping coordinate positions, since only the information from the last loaded form will remain.

The scrolling option of the SAVE command allows you to display one file name at a time. You invoke the scroll by typing a return instead of a file name. Pressing the right arrow key will scroll additional file names.

Saving to Diskette (/SS)   You can save files to diskette by typing

> /SS file name

If the file name you select refers to a file already on the disk, the following prompt will appear:

> FILE EXISTS: TYPE Y TO DELETE

This will have the effect of replacing the old file with the new.

As previously discussed, you can also use the scrolling option with the SAVE command. You can use the file name selected with the scroll as is, thereby resulting in a file replacement, or, you can change the file name by editing with the escape key. This will create a new file. As shown below this provides a convenient way to form a series of related files.

Example:

> Type /SS followed by a return. The first diskette file title will appear on the display. A series of right arrows will display additional file names. Let's assume that the last file is named SALES3.VC and that you wish to create SALES4.VC.
>
> To create SALES4.VC, you use the normal editing capabilities to change the 3 to a 4. Then you press return. This will add SALES4.VC to the diskette.

Deleting Files (/SD)   deletes a named file from a diskette. You may either type in the file name or select it by using the scrolling option.

Quitting VisiCalc (/SQ)   provides a way of returning to the computer's main operating system. To return to the operating system, place an operating system diskette in the disk drive and type /SQ. Memory will be cleared and the operating system will be loaded.

Saving in DIF Format (/S#S)   The standard *data interchange format* (DIF) provides a way of exchanging data between different VisiCalc spreadsheets, and between other programs that use the DIF.

You can specify and save a rectangular area of a spreadsheet. Data and labels are saved in full precision; formulas and expressions are not saved. To use this command, you:

1. place the cursor at the upper left area of the rectangle to be saved.

2. type /S#S *file name.*

3. type the lower right coordinate.

4. type R or C, to specify whether the rectangle is saved in row or column order.

Loading (/S#L)   Loads files already in the DIF. It is not necessary to load files in the same rectangular area or with the same row or column orientation. Thus, a row saved from one spreadsheet may be loaded as a column onto another spreadsheet. To load a DIF file, you:

1. position the cursor at the upper left of the rectangle to be loaded

2. type /S#L file name.

3. type R or C to specify row or column order.

THE TITLES COMMAND

SYNTAX: /T (H,V,B,N)

To help you view a report on the computer screen, VisiCalc will "scroll" the data as you move the cursor from one column or row to another. The TITLES command causes a portion of the screen to remain fixed in place; this allows you to continuously view the label, as you scroll the data.

/TH—causes all the rows at and above the position of the cursor to remain in place. For column labels to remain at the top of the screen, scroll the title row to the top of the screen, using the cursor controls.

/TV— causes all columns at and to the left of the cursor to remain in place.

/TB— combines the effects of the two previous commands. This allows both horizontal and vertical labels to remain fixed.

/TN—returns the screen to its normal appearance.

THE WINDOW COMMAND

SYNTAX: /W (H,V,1,S,U)

This command splits the screen horizontally or vertically at the cursor position, thus developing two windows. You can display the different windows in different global formats. When operating with two windows, you can type a semicolon to move the cursor from one window to another.

/WH—splits the screen into two horizontal windows, just above the row containing the cursor.

/WV—splits the screen just to the left of the column containing the cursor.

/W1—returns to the normal one window condition.

/WS—if two windows are selected, they will initially be scrolled independently. Using this command you can scroll the windows together.

/WU—returns to unsynchronized scrolling.

APPENDIX B: THE VISICALC ADVANCED VERSION

The purpose of this appendix is to discuss the new VisiCalc Advanced Version and its relationship to the applications developed in this book. The VisiCalc Advanced Version is a new program that is upward compatible with earlier versions of VisiCalc; that is, spreadsheets that were developed with the original VisiCalc program will also run on the VisiCalc Advanced Version.

Since the new advanced version requires substantially more memory to operate than the original version, we expect that both versions of the program will continue to be used. It should be noted that spreadsheets developed using the special features of the VisiCalc Advanced Version will not work with the original version of VisiCalc.

We will now discuss some of the important new features offered by this new program.

FINANCIAL FUNCTIONS

The VisiCalc Advanced Version has a number of new financial functions that can help you prepare spreadsheets more quickly. One such function, the INTERNAL RATE OF RETURN function, allows you to calculate the internal rate of return for an investment and its resulting cash flows without using the iterative process that we discussed in Chapter 3. You can easily modify your existing spreadsheets to use this new function.

A second useful function is the PAYMENT function. By simply specifying the interest rate, time period, and present value for a loan, the PAYMENT function will then compute a payment schedule necessary to amortize the loan. In Chapter 7 we provided a formula that will compute this payment; however, you can now simply substitute the PAYMENT function for this formula. In addition, the VisiCalc Advanced Version also has several related functions that will compute interest rates and the present and future values of a series of payments.

CALENDAR FUNCTIONS

The VisiCalc Advanced Version also supports a number of calendar functions that are not available in the original VisiCalc program. These functions allow you to calculate days between dates—a calculation that is necessary in order to calculate yields on some investments. The calendar functions are useful for setting up spreadsheets for short term investments.

There are also a series of functions that you can use to convert hours, minutes, and seconds into fractions of a day.

FORMATTING FUNCTIONS

A new series of formatting functions is available in the VisiCalc Advanced Version that allows you to design even more attractive reports. You may want to go back to some of the spreadsheets we developed in this book and incorporate some of these new features.

One example of the new formatting capability is the ATTRI-BUTE command. This command offers a number of options. For example, let's assume that you are preparing a financial report and you wish to enclose all negative numbers in parentheses. You can do this by moving the cursor to the coordinate of interest and typing /AV(. The VisiCalc program will then enclose all negative numbers in that position in parentheses. Similarly, by using the

/AVC command you can cause positive numbers to be preceded by a CR and negative numbers by a DR. In other words, this command will assign an "attribute" to the coordinate on which you have used the ATTRIBUTE command. You can replicate attributes in the same way that you replicate formats.

Other useful attributes include /AV, which places a comma between the thousand places in numbers, and /AV%, which converts a number to a percentage form and appends a percent sign. Many of the spreadsheets in this book use percentages; you go back and use the /AV% command in the coordinate locations that contain percents. However, be sure to eliminate the division by 100 that we previously added to these coordinates.

Another useful feature of the VisiCalc Advanced Version is that it can maintain differing column widths. For many of the spreadsheets in the book we have provided labels that have extended across two columns. Recall that when we entered these labels onto the spreadsheets, we had to take care to move the cursor to the second column when the first column became filled. With the new SINGLE COLUMN command it is easier to make the column width wider; this, in turn, makes label entry much easier.

PRINTING

The VisiCalc Advanced Version has a number of new features that allow you to print multiple page reports. These features allow you to specify page width and length; they also number pages, and print column and row titles on each page of a multipage report.

BIBLIOGRAPHY

Emory, C. William. *Business Research Methods*. Homewood, Illinois: Richard Irwin, 1976.

Hergert, Douglas. *Mastering VisiCalc*. Berkeley, California: Sybex, Inc., 1982.

Hunt, Pearson; Williams, Charles; and Donaldson, Gordon. *Basic Business Finance*. Homewood, Illinois: Richard Irwin, 1971.

Kernighan, Brian W., and Plauger, P. J. *The Elements of Programming Style*. New York: McGraw-Hill, 1974.

Laufer, Arthur. *Operations Management*. Cincinatti, Ohio: South-Western Publishing Co., 1975.

Levin, Richard I., and Kirkpatrick, Charles. *Quantitative Approaches to Management*. New York: McGraw-Hill, 1978.

Parket, I. Robert. *Statistics for Business Decision Making*. New York: Random House, 1974.

Pyle, William; White, John; and Larson, Kermit. *Fundamental Accounting Principles*. Homewood, Illinois: Richard Irwin, 1978.

Van Tassel, Dennie. *Program Style, Design, Efficiency, Debugging, and Testing*. Englewood Cliffs, New Jersey: Prentice-Hall, 1978.

Weston, J. Fred, and Brigham, Eugene. *Managerial Finance*. Hinsdale, Illinois: Dryden Press, 1978.

INDEX

The SYBEX Library

GENERAL INTEREST

DON'T (or How to Care for Your Computer)
by Rodnay Zaks 214 pp., 100 illustr., Ref. 0-065

The correct way to handle and care for all elements of a computer system, including what to do when something doesn't work.

YOUR FIRST COMPUTER
by Rodnay Zaks 258 pp., 150 illustr., Ref. 0-045

The most popular introduction to small computers and their peripherals: what they do and how to buy one.

INTERNATIONAL MICROCOMPUTER DICTIONARY
120 pp., Ref. 0-067

All the definitions and acronyms of microcomputer jargon defined in a handy pocket-size edition. Includes translations of the most popular terms into ten languages.

THE BEST OF CP/M® SOFTWARE
by Alan R. Miller 250 pp., illustr., Ref. 0-100

This book reviews tried-and-tested, commercially available software for your CP/M system.

FOR YOUR IBM PC

USEFUL BASIC PROGRAMS FOR THE IBM® PC
by Stanley R. Trost 174 pp., illustr., Ref. 0-111

A collection of programs for making financial calculations, analyzing investments, keeping records, and many more home, office and school applications.

IBM® PC DOS HANDBOOK
by Richard King 144 pp., illustr., Ref. 0-103

Explains the PC disk operating system, giving the user better control over the system. Get the most out of your PC by adapting its capabilities to your specific needs.

FOR YOUR TIMEX SINCLAIR 1000/ZX81™

YOUR TIMEX SINCLAIR 1000™ AND ZX81™
by Douglas Hergert 159 pp., illustr., Ref. 0-099

This book explains the set-up, operation, and capabilities of the Timex Sinclair 1000 and ZX81. Includes how to interface peripheral devices, and introduces BASIC programming.

THE TIMEX SINCLAIR 1000™ BASIC HANDBOOK
by Douglas Hergert 170 pp., illustr. Ref. 0-113
A complete alphabetical listing with explanations and examples of each word in the TS 1000 BASIC vocabulary; will allow you quick, error free programming of your TS 1000.

TIMEX SINCLAIR 1000™ BASIC PROGRAMS IN MINUTES
by Stanley R. Trost 150 pp., illustr., Ref. 0-119
A collection of ready-to-run programs for financial calculations, investment analysis, record keeping, and many more home and office applications. These programs can be entered on your TS 1000 in minutes!

FOR YOUR TRS-80

YOUR COLOR COMPUTER
by Doug Mosher 350 pp., illustr., Ref. 0-097
Patience and humor guide the reader through purchasing, setting up, programming, and using the Radio Shack TRS-80/TDP Series 100 Color Computer. A complete introduction to the color computer.

THE FOOLPROOF GUIDE TO SCRIPSIT™ WORD PROCESSING
by Jeff Berner 225 pp., illustr., Ref. 0-098
Everything you need to know about SCRIPSIT—from starting out, to mastering document editing. This user-friendly guide is written in plain English, with a touch of wit.

FOR YOUR APPLE

THE APPLE® CONNECTION
by James W. Coffron 264 pp., 120 illustr., Ref. 0-085
Teaches elementary interfacing and BASIC programming of the Apple for connection to external devices and household appliances.

BUSINESS & PROFESSIONAL

INTRODUCTION TO WORD PROCESSING
by Hal Glatzer 205 pp., 140 illustr., Ref. 0-076
Explains in plain language what a word processor can do, how it improves productivity, how to use a word processor and how to buy one wisely.

INTRODUCTION TO WORDSTAR™
by Arthur Naiman 202 pp., 30 illustr., Ref. 0-077
Makes it easy to learn how to use WordStar, a powerful word processing program for personal computers.

PRACTICAL WORDSTAR™ USES
by Julie Anne Arca 200 pp., illustr., Ref. 0-107
Special applications for essential office tasks are explained in step-by-step detail. Makes using WordStar efficient and fun.

MASTERING VISICALC®
by Douglas Hergert   217 pp., 140 illustr., Ref. 0-090
Explains how to use the VisiCalc "electronic spreadsheet" functions and provides examples of each. Makes using this powerful program simple.

DOING BUSINESS WITH VISICALC®
by Stanley R. Trost   260 pp., Ref. 0-086
Presents accounting and management planning applications—from financial statements to master budgets; from pricing models to investment strategies.

DOING BUSINESS WITH SUPERCALC™
by Stanley R. Trost   248 pp., illustr., Ref. 0-095
Presents accounting and management planning applications—from financial statements to master budgets; from pricing models to investment strategies. This is for computers with CP/M.

VISICALC® FOR SCIENCE AND ENGINEERING
by Stanley R. Trost & Charles Pomernacki   225 pp., illustr., Ref. 0-096
More than 50 programs for solving technical problems in the science and engineering fields. Applications range from math and statistics to electrical and electronic engineering.

BASIC

FIFTY BASIC EXERCISES
by J. P. Lamoitier   232 pp., 90 illustr., Ref. 0-056
Teaches BASIC by actual practice, using graduated exercises drawn from everyday applications. All programs written in Microsoft BASIC.

BASIC EXERCISES FOR THE APPLE®
by J. P. Lamoitier   250 pp., 90 illustr., Ref. 0-084
This book is an Apple version of *Fifty BASIC Exercises.*

BASIC EXERCISES FOR THE IBM® PERSONAL COMPUTER
by J. P. Lamoitier   252 pp., 90 illustr., Ref. 0-088
This book is an IBM version of *Fifty BASIC Exercises.*

BASIC EXERCISES FOR THE ATARI®
by J.P. Lamoitier   251 pp., illustr., Ref. 0-101
This is the ATARI version of *Fifty BASIC Exercises.*

INSIDE BASIC GAMES
by Richard Mateosian   348 pp., 120 illustr., Ref. 0-055
Teaches interactive BASIC programming through games. Games are written in Microsoft BASIC and can run on the TRS-80, Apple II and PET/CBM.

YOUR FIRST BASIC PROGRAM
by Rodnay Zaks   150 pp., illustr., Ref. 0-092
A fully illustrated, easy-to-use, introduction to BASIC programming. Will have the reader programming in a matter of hours.

BASIC FOR BUSINESS
by Douglas Hergert   224 pp., 15 illustr., Ref. 0-080
A logically organized, no-nonsense introduction to BASIC programming for business applications. Includes many fully-explained accounting programs, and shows you how to write them.

EXECUTIVE PLANNING WITH BASIC
by X. T. Bui   196 pp., 19 illustr., Ref. 0-083
An important collection of business management decision models in BASIC, including Inventory Management (EOQ), Critical Path Analysis and PERT, Financial Ratio Analysis, Portfolio Management, and much more.

BASIC PROGRAMS FOR SCIENTISTS AND ENGINEERS
by Alan R. Miller   318 pp., 120 illustr., Ref. 0-073
This second book in the "Programs for Scientists and Engineers" series provides a library of problem-solving programs while developing proficiency in BASIC.

CELESTIAL BASIC: Astronomy on Your Computer
by Eric Burgess   300 pp., 65 illustr., Ref. 0-087
A collection of BASIC programs that rapidly complete the chores of typical astronomical computations. It's like having a planetarium in your own home! Displays apparent movement of stars, planets and meteor showers.

PASCAL

INTRODUCTION TO PASCAL (Including UCSD Pascal™)
by Rodnay Zaks   420 pp., 130 illustr., Ref. 0-066
A step-by-step introduction for anyone wanting to learn the Pascal language. Describes UCSD and Standard Pascals. No technical background is assumed.

THE PASCAL HANDBOOK
by Jacques Tiberghien   486 pp., 270 illustr., Ref. 0-053
A dictionary of the Pascal language, defining every reserved word, operator, procedure and function found in all major versions of Pascal.

APPLE® PASCAL GAMES
by Douglas Hergert and Joseph T. Kalash   372 pp., 40 illustr., Ref. 0-074
A collection of the most popular computer games in Pascal, challenging the reader not only to play but to investigate how games are implemented on the computer.

INTRODUCTION TO THE UCSD p-SYSTEM™
by Charles W. Grant and Jon Butah   300 pp., 10 illustr., Ref. 0-061
A simple, clear introduction to the UCSD Pascal Operating System; for beginners through experienced programmers.

PASCAL PROGRAMS FOR SCIENTISTS AND ENGINEERS
by Alan R. Miller   374 pp., 120 illustr., Ref. 0-058
A comprehensive collection of frequently used algorithms for scientific and technical applications, programmed in Pascal. Includes such programs as curve-fitting, integrals and statistical techniques.

DOING BUSINESS WITH PASCAL
by Richard Hergert & Douglas Hergert   371 pp., illustr., Ref. 0-091
Practical tips for using Pascal in business programming. Includes design considerations, language extensions, and applications examples.

OTHER LANGUAGES

FORTRAN PROGRAMS FOR SCIENTISTS AND ENGINEERS
by Alan R. Miller   280 pp., 120 illustr., Ref. 0-082
Third in the "Programs for Scientists and Engineers" series. Specific scientific and engineering application programs written in FORTRAN.

A MICROPROGRAMMED APL IMPLEMENTATION
by Rodnay Zaks   350 pp., Ref. 0-005
An expert-level text presenting the complete conceptual analysis and design of an APL interpreter, and actual listing of the microcode.

CP/M

THE CP/M® HANDBOOK
by Rodnay Zaks   320 pp., 100 illustr., Ref. 0-048
An indispensable reference and guide to CP/M—the most widely-used operating system for small computers.

MASTERING CP/M®
by Alan R. Miller   398 pp., Ref. 0-068
For advanced CP/M users or systems programmers who want maximum use of the CP/M operating system ... takes up where our *CP/M Handbook* leaves off.

ASSEMBLY LANGUAGE PROGRAMMING

PROGRAMMING THE 6502
by Rodnay Zaks   386 pp., 160 illustr., Ref. 0-046
Assembly language programming for the 6502, from basic concepts to advanced data structures.

6502 APPLICATIONS
by Rodnay Zaks   278 pp., 200 illustr., Ref. 0-015
Real-life application techniques: the input/output book for the 6502.

ADVANCED 6502 PROGRAMMING
by Rodnay Zaks   292 pp., 140 illustr., Ref. 0-089
Third in the 6502 series. Teaches more advanced programming techniques, using games as a framework for learning.

PROGRAMMING THE Z80
by Rodnay Zaks   624 pp., 200 illustr., Ref. 0-069
A complete course in programming the Z80 microprocessor and a thorough introduction to assembly language.

Z80 APPLICATIONS
by James W. Coffron   288 pp., illustr., Ref. 0-094
Covers techniques and applications for using peripheral devices with a Z80 based system.

PROGRAMMING THE 6809
by Rodnay Zaks and William Labiak   362 pp., 150 illustr., Ref. 0-078
This book explains how to program the 6809 in assembly language. No prior programming knowledge required.

PROGRAMMING THE Z8000
by Richard Mateosian   298 pp., 124 illustr., Ref. 0-032
How to program the Z8000 16-bit microprocessor. Includes a description of the architecture and function of the Z8000 and its family of support chips.

HARDWARE

MICROPROCESSOR INTERFACING TECHNIQUES
by Rodnay Zaks and Austin Lesea   456 pp., 400 illustr., Ref. 0-029
Complete hardware and software interconnect techniques, including D to A conversion, peripherals, standard buses and troubleshooting.

FROM CHIPS TO SYSTEMS:
AN INTRODUCTION TO MICROPROCESSORS
by Rodnay Zaks   552 pp., 400 illustr., Ref. 0-063
A simple and comprehensive introduction to microprocessors from both a hardware and software standpoint: what they are, how they operate, how to assemble them into a complete system.

FOR A COMPLETE CATALOG
OF OUR PUBLICATIONS

U.S.A.
2344 Sixth Street
Berkeley,
California 94710
Tel: (415) 848-8233
Telex: 336311

SYBEX-EUROPE
4 Place Félix-Eboué
75583 Paris Cedex 12
France
Tel: 1/347-30-20
Telex: 211801

SYBEX-VERLAG
Heyestr. 22
4000 Düsseldorf 12
West Germany
Tel: (0211) 287066
Telex: 08 588 163

SYBEX® COMPUTERBOOKS

are different.

Here is why . . .

At SYBEX, each book is designed with you in mind. Every manuscript is carefully selected and supervised by our editors, who are themselves computer experts. Programs are thoroughly tested for accuracy by our technical staff. Our computerized production department goes to great lengths to make sure that each book is designed as well as it is written. We publish the finest authors, whose technical expertise is matched by an ability to write clearly and to communicate effectively.

In the pursuit of timeliness, SYBEX has achieved many publishing firsts. SYBEX was among the first to integrate personal computers used by authors and staff into the publishing process. SYBEX was the first to publish books on the CP/M operating system, microprocessor interfacing techniques, word processing, and many more topics.

Expertise in computers and dedication to the highest quality in book publishing have made SYBEX a world leader in microcomputer education. Translated into fourteen languages, SYBEX books have helped millions of people around the world to get the most from their computers. We hope we have helped you, too.